SELF-PORTRAIT IN APOLOGIES

AND OTHER ESSAYS

Sarah Einstein

Copyright © 2025 by Sarah Einstein

Excerpts from this book may be reproduced for reviews and quotations for fair use in a classroom. To obtain permission to reprint, or otherwise reproduce or distribute material from this book, please contact the Press at msp1@mountainstatepress.org.

ISBN: 978-1-7351635-8-1

Cover and interior design: Morgan Barchett
Line editing/copy editing: Michele Schiavone
Editor-in-chief: Cat Pleska

Acknowledgments for previously published material appears at the back of the book.

Mountain State Press

www.mountainstatepress.org
In collaboration with Marshall University

CONTENTS

DEDICATION v

Self-Portrait in Apologies 7

The Origins of My Problems with Fidelity 15

A Meditation on Love 17

Fearsome Beauty 25

The Way Things Go 35

Almost Home 51

Shelter 63

What I Know of Madness 75

When I Lived in Manhattan 89

Mot 95

Going to Ground 121

On Marriage 125

Striking the Match 127

A Young Man Tells Me 133

DEDICATION

To Dominik, to whom I rarely apologize because he has taught me how to be careful with one another instead.

Self-Portrait in Apologies

Apology to an Ethically Inconsistent Friend

I'm sorry for picking the chicken out of the soup and telling you it was vegetarian. I was broke and there wasn't anything else in the house to offer you. Besides, the last time I saw you, you were eating a cheeseburger and smoking a Marlboro.

Apology to Three Lovers from My Youth

I'm sorry for telling you I was a virgin that night in the back of your car. In your parents' basement. In my dorm room. As you may have guessed years ago, I wasn't.

Apology to the Boy Who Wasn't Quite Right

Even in the comparatively egalitarian world of first grade, it was social suicide to be seen with you on the playground. Until third grade, you were The Boy Our Parents Made Us Be Nice To, the one who was invited to birthday parties and sat in a corner, alone except when our mothers dragged you out of your chair to play some game they rigged so you could win.

It wasn't until we were almost ready for junior high that we realized you'd started to disappear. Your skin became translucent, like the skin of the dead goldfish floating at the top of a tank. You stopped talking, and it seemed your parents kept you home more days than they allowed you to come to school. If we hadn't stopped noticing you years before, maybe it would have occurred to us that something was wrong, but I doubt it. We were safe children whose understanding of danger didn't extend beyond the laughing, swinging-too-high, running-too-fast sort.

At some point, you disappeared altogether. I vaguely remember thinking you were away at a boarding school for frighteningly smart children, but that may have been someone else.

It wasn't until years later that we learned your scoutmaster had raped you almost daily. You weren't the only boy, of course, but for almost a decade you were his favorite. I like to believe that, had we known, we'd have rallied behind you and launched some sort of children's crusade to protect you. But, really, I'm certain we would have seen it as just one more reason to avoid you. I'm sorry.

Apology to a Friend with a Difficult Love Life

There wasn't someone at the door; it's just that you had gone on and on about what a jerk your new boyfriend had turned out to be, and I had better things to do. Had I listened to you for one more minute, I would have said, "Look, you're only dating him. If he's such a jerk, move on. You do this every time." Instead, I rang my own doorbell. I'm sorry.

The First Ghost Who Lingers, Waiting for an Apology

An old woman I didn't know—the grandmother of a friend—reached up toward the sound of my cough and muttered *Who are you* and *Where am I* as I witnessed the spectacle of her death. I'm sorry for intruding on a moment I had no right to attend.

Apology to a Man I No Longer Love

I'm sorry for hiding your favorite Leonard Cohen CD in the bottom of a box of tampons when we were dividing up our stuff after the breakup. I still have it, all these years later, and sometimes forget it wasn't a gift from you.

Apology to a Well-Meaning History Teacher

We were as cruel as 13-year-olds usually are, and didn't care that you'd escaped a World War by hiding in the dank basement of a strange family's house. We laughed at your accent but didn't listen to your stories about surviving on rotting apples and hard, brown bread. We hid your glasses when you stepped out of the classroom, as you often did, to hike up the pants of your ill-fitting suits that shone at elbow, knee, and seat. We rearranged ourselves with utter disregard for your seating chart, knowing you could not tell if we had moved or you had simply grown confused. We laughed at everything except your small jokes meant to show that you, too, knew you'd grown a little pathetic and befuddled. Instead, we whispered *Creepy old man* to one another behind our pink, uncalloused hands on which we'd inscribed the names of Renaissance artists, just in case there was a quiz.

Apology to Everyone in the Dress Row at the Metropolitan Opera, Seats 114–120, on October 13, 1995

When I woke up with a hacking cough and runny nose, I thought only, "These tickets cost a fortune" and "I'll never get another chance to see Plácido Domingo sing *Otello*." I didn't think of how my constant sniffling and wheezing would ruin your evening. And, to the lady in seat 118, my particular apology for sneezing so emphatically that I caused you to drop your opera glasses onto a gentleman in the Grand Tier. I hope no one was hurt, and that you were able to retrieve them after the curtain fell. They looked expensive, and heavy enough to raise a good-sized lump.

Apology to the Woman Whose Dog I Couldn't Love

It's not that he wasn't a good boy, I'm sure he was. It was that I couldn't understand why you'd let him in bed with us, or how you could still be passionate while he looked on, his basset hound eyes more full of remorse than curiosity.

Apology to the Man I Hit with My "Peace in the Middle East" Protest Sign at the Antiwar Rally in DC on March 26, 1991

I didn't see you until after I felt your hand on my arm, pulling me out of the phalanx of marchers armed with placards and chanting our way down Pennsylvania Avenue. *The people, united, will never be defeated* and *What do we want? Peace! When do we want it? Now!* I was hopped up on adrenaline, a sense of moral certainty, and the bourbon Paula and I were passing between us to fight off the cold. I was marching, and then out of nowhere you were pulling me out of the ranks and shouting at me that I was to blame for every one of our soldiers who died because I was a goddamned bleeding-heart liberal. It scared me, and before I knew what I was doing I felt the thud of your skull against the two-by-four to which I'd stapled my peace sign. I am sorry for the bloody gash across your forehead, and for making you think you'd been proven right.

In This Story, Christmas Past Is the Second Ghost

The Peters boy died on Christmas Eve in 1977, his head in our yard, his body still in his brand-new convertible; the top down in spite of the snow. The drunk who hit him was yelling, "You cut me off, you little shit" at the dead boy. I watched for a while from my bedroom, the scene strobing off and on with the blinking Christmas lights that framed my window and then went back to bed.

What I remember most about that Christmas is the Major League Baseball pinball machine from my father, with real bumpers and a slot for the quarters it no longer needed. My brothers and I loved that pinball machine, and all the younger kids in the neighborhood spent Christmas Day at our house, trying for the high score and looking out the window at the torn-up patch of lawn and the blood in the snow.

I'm sorry for being part of the crowd that stood away from your younger brother at the bus stop when school started again, shuffling my feet and looking down whenever he glanced at me from his lonely post by the stop sign.

Apology to the Woman I Slept with Twice Too Often

I understood by then that we had no actual future; you'd exchanged your feminist t-shirts and embroidery thread jewelry for button downs and brogues, I'd just pierced my nose and was contemplating a tattoo. I knew you were only sleeping with me because you hoped it meant we could try again. I was only sleeping with you so that I didn't have to say, out loud, that we had already gone too far down diverging roads.

Apology to the Man Whose Woods We Burned Down

We were 14 years old and brave in that stupid teenage way, learning to smoke and flicking lit matches into a wet pile of leaves in the woods behind your house. Fifteen minutes later, we were back in Donna's room, pretending to only then be getting up for the day, and heard sirens wailing closer and closer until they Dopplered past her house. The street was a dead end; they could only be going to the woods. We yawned in our little-girl pajamas and asked her mother what was going on. "Oh, some vagrants caught the woods on fire," she said. We asked for pancakes and plopped down in front of the television, laughing in that stoned teenage way as we watched *Scooby-Doo*, worried about getting caught but not about whether or not we had done something wrong.

Both you and Donna are dead, so maybe there isn't any point in apologizing. Still, I wish you could see the hillside now. With the pine all burned away, it has become a Georgia O'Keeffe explosion of pastel mountain laurel; in the spring, it stands out among the scraggly evergreens like a swath of virgin-pink lipstick.

The Third Ghost, Because in Literature There Are Always Three Ghosts

I met Great-Aunt Bethel, with her shriveled hands and sunken cheeks, in a nursing home when I was ten. She held my arm with surprising strength and begged, over and over again, "Please get me out of here." Finally, a nurse pried Bethel's fingers from around my wrist and took me outside to the horse they had stabled in the backyard. When Bethel died, a year later, my father said, "Well, it's not like anyone is going to cry over her grave," and laughed. I'm sorry for not understanding that it wasn't a joke, and for laughing as if it were.

Apology to the Spider I Killed in the Bathtub, Even Though I Tell People I Don't Kill Spiders

I was already naked, and you were bigger and more menacing than the simple brown house spiders that usually crawl down from the attic. I should have cupped you into a water glass and carried you safely to the garden, but you looked poisonous and I needed to get into the shower. You died because I overslept.

Apology to an Accidental Cannibal

We were docked for every sandwich we wasted, and it was only a minimum wage job. So when I noticed that I had sliced off a thin layer of skin along the backhand edge of my right hand, and that the flesh and fatty tissue had fallen into your roast beef sandwich, I just slapped some American cheese over it and served it to you anyway. I am sorry for not telling you, and also for telling the other girls at the counter once you were safely seated and chomping away and I had a rag tied around my hand. You must have wondered why we kept looking at you, laughing, and then doing the stiff-legged zombie walk up and down the service area. "Brains," we said, "must eat brains. Or hand sandwiches."

Apology to the Birds We No Longer Feed

After you ate the sweet inside of the nuts and seeds, the rats gathered for the bitter husks.

Apology to My Martyred Forebears

When Christmastime rolls around, someone always says to me, "You know, you had family that died in the Holocaust because of their faith. How do you think they'd feel if they saw you in this Mennonite church of yours? Don't you ever think of them?"

And I say, "Which holocaust was that? There are so many."

But, in truth, I think of you all the time. I picture you miserable in some version of the Hereafter that fits neither my old nor my new religion but looks something like a bus station in Eastern Europe. You are dressed in drab, damp coats and eating greasy food from rolled-up newspapers. Your eyes are tired, your bodies lumpen and dirty. You are the miserable dead, and I am your misery. Years from now, I will go to look for the home you left in Lithuania and, there, find unreadable graves where some of you must rest, and those graves will remind me who I am. I am sorry for my thousand betrayals. Forgive me.

The Origins of My Problems with Fidelity

The tender young men with their brand new lankiness and downy chin hair stood in a circle, shuffling from foot to foot in the cold, chanting *fight, fight, fight*. The lankiest, most awkward boy of all held the center, arms akimbo, yelling above the chorus *Come on, you stupid dyke, you want a piece of me? Mess with my girlfriend? Come on, you want to be a man? Then be a man.* Though nobody there was a man; the oldest of us was fifteen. The girl, who was stocky and stronger than any of them, threw the first punch. She said *I'm a damn sight better man than you'll ever be Frank Adkins and I will kiss whoever I want* as her fist knocked hard against his jaw. *There will never be a girl who would rather kiss you than me* as she shoved a shoulder into his belly. *You don't want to mess with me asshole* as he fell to the ground.

This is how I came to believe, wrongly, that she was my girlfriend. When she had kissed me at the concert, we'd been forbidden to attend, her lips sticky with Boones Farm, I thought it was in spite of the fact that I was sort of Frank Adkins' girlfriend, not because of it. But she hadn't wanted to kiss me except to prove a point to him, to finally have a reason to pound his ass into the black tar asphalt of the playground in retribution for the way he'd tormented her since her parents kicked her out of the house for being *unnatural* when we were all in sixth grade.

I picked up her discarded jacket and hat and came toward her after the fight, feeling the complicated warmth of a girl who has just been fought over. She said only *what the hell do you think you're doing with my stuff* and *give me that right now* and *this has nothing to do with you.* Not *let me walk you home* or *do you want to go to the dance?* Not *will you be my girlfriend* or *do you want to go steady?* But still, her eye was blackened and she had kissed me, so it took me a while to understand.

For weeks, I sent her love notes on lined notebook paper folded into swans and boats. She sent these back to me with the words *you're so gay* or *leave me the hell alone* scrawled across them.

And so I let Frank Adkins take me to the ninth grade dance, let him grind his tiny, teenage boy erection against my thigh during the slow songs, let him kiss me in the dark hallway between the gymnasium and the bathrooms, let him put a hand on my breast over my blouse. It was disappointing and a little gross, his tongue in my mouth like a piece of under cooked meat, but I was a girl of fourteen for whom being a person that someone wanted to kiss mattered more than who that someone was. The ugly girl late to the party, the fat girl dancing by herself under the crepe paper and balloons, the awkward girl in the back brace pretending that I, too, thought it was funny when they knocked my books out of my arms so they could watch me get down on my belly to gather them. But, at least, no longer the one girl who had never been kissed. Not so broken and awful as that.

A Meditation on Love

Mommy Buddha is grousing again, hitching up his skirts and planting his big, black Chuck Taylors into the rutted mud of the road. His backpack rests heavy on my shoulders—he is done with carrying it, he's insisted with a snap of the finger and a waggle of the head that isn't, here in 1987, yet a cultural marker that's moved far beyond the drag community.

"Fucking hippies," he says as we reach the end of Bus Village, where the old naked guy at the hard road had told us we would find Hippie Hollow, the part of the Rainbow Gathering where we intended to camp. "There isn't anything here. It's just a dead end."

I cajole him into moving on, the way one might a small child, with promises of a warm, dry place to pitch our tent and get some sleep. Mommy Buddha is not a small child; he's a six foot three, three hundred pound Philosophy student and a man tough enough to wear housedresses and a blond topknot to class at the University of Alabama. But he's also not not a child, with his tantrums and his quivery lower lip and his life-is-so-unfairing. I don't want to spend the night in the muck of the road, or the swampy dead end of it, and I am able to keep him moving because he is a creature of comforts.

So we trek down the road again, and up another branch off it for a while, Mommy Buddha muttering under his breath. And then, as if there actually was something to this Rainbow Family magic, to this once-a-year-moveable-magic-love-in, I hear a voice I know. And that voice is telling a story I know, the one about

Thanksgiving at his parents' farm, his father complaining about at the words we're using on the Scrabble board, words he doesn't know, words like textual and orality which he says don't sound like good Christian words to him and talking about don't talk that college talk in my house son, and talking about too big for our britches, and talking about getting above our raising. I know this story because I was there.

So Mommy Buddha and I stop.

And it turns out that the voice belongs to Terry-who-was-my-boyfriend-before-that-awful-business-with-the-cops-and-the-weed, and he says, "Okay, then, you can sleep in my tent," to Mommy Buddha and "Here, take this" to me and I do take this, which is a cup of hot tea that turns out to have mushrooms in it but I don't know that, I think it's just a cup of tea at the end of a long journey.

And then I'm sitting by the fire listening to stories about people I think but am not sure that I knew once, a long time ago, even though I've never met the people who are telling these stories before, and Terry-who-was-my-boyfriend-before-that-awful-business-with-the-cops-and-the-weed is braiding my hair into a hundred tiny braids down my back, weaving in pieces of embroidery thread and tiny silver bells and vine. And because I don't know that there are mushrooms in the tea, for the next couple of hours I think maybe the warm feeling in my belly, the loveliness of the faces of the familiar strangers around the campfire, the joyful tinkling of the bells in my hair mean that I'm still in love with Terry-who-was-my-boyfriend-before-that-awful-business-with-the-cops-and-the-weed. That maybe this whole magical Rainbow Gathering moment is meant to show me that he is my soul mate and that I should say everything is forgiven and forgive me and we should try again. But right before I make a fool of myself, I notice that I'm getting tracers off the joint that the familiar strangers are now passing amongst them and I ask, "Was this tea dosed?" "Just 'shrooms," says a girl in a Ramones t-shirt and a The Cat in the Hat hat, and I realize I'm just buzzed, and not still in love with Terry-who-was-my-boyfriend-before-that-awful-business-with-the-cops-and-the-weed, which is a relief, because the friends who lived through that-awful-business-with-the-cops-and-the-weed would not be pleased to hear that he was once again Terry-who-is-my-boyfriend. And, really, they'd be right.

Besides, it would have created pretty significant problems with Dogman-who-is-my-boyfriend-now.

In the morning Mommy Buddha and I take our backpacks and find Hippie Hollow proper. We camp among some students from Kent who are here on a sort of combined peace mission/drug run that never fully makes sense to me. Mommy Buddha spends much of the time running into town to buy fast food; he has Crohn's Disease and can't take the whole-grain, raw-vegetable, everything-spiced-with-garlic-and-hot-pepper-sauce food that is served up at the free kitchens around the gathering. So he wakes up, walks the few miles to the car, drives into town, and sits at McDonald's during the heat of the day, and then drives back in the evening. He's already disgusted with the dirt and the lack of queer boys with ponytails who he'd hoped would want to have sex with him.

I spend the days wandering around just staring at stuff: the giant spider webs woven into jungle gyms by the noncompetitive play folk, the painted elephant that the Krishnas brought from New Vrindaban, the jugglers and giant bubble blowers and dervishes whirling in the dust.

At night I lay in our borrowed tent and listen to the echoing, sing-songy we love yous that float through the hills. I call back until Mommy Buddha tells me that if I don't shut the hell up and let him sleep he's going to show me how much he does not love all this hippie bullshit in his mean voice, and then I just lay there quietly feeling all that echoing love wash over me. Because, although I know it's hokey and more than a little played out, I actually believe in the power of love, organic vegetable curry over brown rice, dreadlocks, and drum circles to change the world. I believe those strangers up in the hills when they holler into the night we love you the way my Christian friends believe Jesus loves them.

I'm twenty-one and have just figured out how alone I really am in the world, that I don't belong to my parents any more, that I will make it or not based solely on what I can and choose to do. That it is, in fact, possible not to make it, to auger in and fall apart and wind up spending most evenings alone in your apartment eating green beans out of the can and listening to Joni Mitchell before just going the hell to bed at nine o'clock because there isn't any reason not to and you have to work tomorrow anyway.

So, I really want to believe that these strangers love me. And they want me to believe it, too. I know they do. Which is why I stay away from Krishna Kitchen, even though they have the most reliably potable water. I recognize that I am, at this moment, lonely in a dangerous way. In a maybe-it-wouldn't-be-so-bad-to-move-to-New-Vrindaban-in-spite-of-the-rumors-of-drug-running-and-underaged-sex-scandals way. Well, that, and there is a persistent rumor that they put saltpeter in their food to help folk avoid the temptations of illicit sex, and I'm pretty okay with giving in to that particular temptation under the right circumstances. Though it might explain why Mommy Buddha is having such a hard time finding pony-tailed boys who want to have sex with him.

We stay through the Om ceremony on the Fourth of July, joining in the chanting of thousands of tie-dyed, shaggy-haired peaceniks in Main Meadow and then erupting into hoots of joy and dancing. Or, at least, I erupt. Mommy Buddha sits with our packed gear and waits for me to get the hell over it so that we can get on the road. On the way to the car, we pass a small booth passing out copies of *AllWays Free*, a sort of newsletter/crash pad guide put together by the Rainbow Family. High on love, and possibly hash from a brownie handed to me by a passing woman in Main Meadow that tasted like dirt and happiness, I put down my name and my address. "Rainbow family all ways welcomed!" I write underneath.

We pile our dirty selves and our dirty gear into Mommy Buddha's old, broken down Volvo on which we had painted My

Car-ma and glued plastic dinosaurs in preparation for our journey. Car drag. I'm dressed in an ugly brown and orange dashiki that I found in a pile of give-aways at one of the kitchens, Mommy Buddha's wearing one of his customary housedresses. So, of course, we get a flat tire. In Alabama. And equally of course, Mommy Buddha doesn't have a jack, though at least he has a spare.

"I'm pretty certain that this is where we get murdered," I say, as we sit by the side of the road. We get flipped off and honked at, but for a very long time nobody is inclined to stop and help.

"Shut up," says Mommy Buddha. "Just shut the fuck up, okay?"

So I do. We're both scared. The only thing worse than having nobody stop to help would be to have a state trooper stop to help and—because I'm wearing a dashiki and he's wearing a housedress and there are plastic dinosaurs glued to the car which most certainly all add up to probable cause—take a little look-see at what all we have in the car. Which, along with all our smelly gear and a week's worth of fast food wrappers, is a sheet of blotter acid and some mighty fine marijuana. The blotter acid is half the reason I went to the gathering, and all the reason Mommy Buddha agreed to come along. Well, that and the ponytailed queer boy sex I'd promised him that had turned out to be a lot harder to find than the drugs. We would throw it away, but there isn't any place to throw it. No woods. Not even any kudzu. Just a flat expanse of concrete and dry packed clay.

And after about an hour I start praying for the murderer to show up before the southern policeman because I'm pretty sure

I'd rather be dead than a Jewish hippie chick locked up in a rural Alabama jail.

Also, I start to wonder how long it takes to die of thirst.

And at pretty much that same moment it occurs to me that maybe I should have looked for Terry-who-was-my-boyfriend-before-that-awful-business-with-the-cops-and-the-weed before we left, and at least said goodbye.

Finally, after we've been sitting in the road dust for a good two and a half hours, a trucker pulls over and changes the tire for us. Actually, he makes a U-turn and comes back to change our tire, because he'd been driving the other way. He makes it known up front that he didn't want to stop, doesn't really like our kind and thinks we're pretty much idiots, but he also either never figures out that we aren't both girls or he does figure it out and has no idea what to make of Mommy Buddha so just pretends to still think we're both girls, and he says he just couldn't feel right about leaving two young girls stranded by the side of the road. He tells us a little bit about what Jesus means to him, but in a way that's lovely and explains why he stopped, not in a way that makes it seem like he might fix the tire and then murder us for being abominations of nature or something. So, we're grateful.

As he pulls away, he says "Jesus loves you, you know." He brakes to give us one last looksee. "Even people like you," he adds.

And after he's gone, I call out in that sing-songy Rainbow way, "We love you!" Mommy Buddha rolls his eyes and pulls out into traffic.

Fearsome Beauty

Morgantown, WV 1992

I have never been able to stand yards, those tiny, cramped plots of grass guarded over by the windows of neighbors. At seven I realized most of my mother's omniscience was in fact simply the work of an elaborate network of spies, women who watched out their kitchen windows ready to phone in the least misdeed. I could feel their eyes forbidding me to venture beyond the strict code of neighborhood law. There was no time when I felt less alone, or more isolated, than when I was playing by myself in the backyard surrounded by the hostile stares of other people's mothers. "Outside" was the most public room in our house.

When I was eight, the gate in the backyard was finally opened and I was given the run of the streets. Once freed from the omnipresence of adults, I lived in a world populated by fairies, ancient Indian tribes, and murderers. Every reclusive old woman became a witch, every abandoned house the site of a brutal massacre. Ant trails in the bark of fallen branches were really cryptic messages sent by a shaman; broken pieces of Melmac dishes abandoned in the alleys were shards of ancient pottery. I created a world of demons and dryads I knew would crumble under the careful scrutiny of adult eyes. I came to covet my aloneness, even shunning the company of other children who would stubbornly insist on seeing only a discarded glass, never a grail.

Now that I am older, I find that I must go even further from home–

and those eyes so filled with judgment–to recreate the world and confront my demons. Each year, as the languor of spring ripens into the lethargy of summer, I make a pilgrimage to Beauty Mountain in central West Virginia. There, amid the teaberry and mountain laurel, I set up my tent on one of the outcroppings overlooking the New River Gorge. Nine hundred feet down–almost straight down–the river tosses fragile rafts back and forth as it rages toward its destination, but on the mountain all is still. I come here to live alone among the snakes and the silence because it frightens me and fear reawakens my senses to the mysteries that surround me.

As I prepare for this, my seventh sojourn to the mountain, I become my own parent. I borrow my father's eyes to crawl under the car and check the brakes, change the oil, gauge the air pressure in my tires, and check the treads. Like my mother, I sit for hours in front of the weather channel, placing my faith in the mystical powers of meteorologists. I ask a neighbor's child to feed the cat and bring in the mail; as he takes his ten dollars he calls me "Mrs. Einstein" though I am single, and I know it is because in his eyes I am old.

Of all the rituals necessary to begin this journey, choosing the contents of my backpack is the most crucial and the most superstitious. If I pack my poncho instead of extra batteries, I can ensure that the weather will be good but my flashlight will die. Having caught on to Nature's contrary psychology, I pack as though headed into the aftermath of some terrible disaster. Over the years, aspirin has replaced alcohol and my *Field Guide to North American Reptiles* the works of Carlos Castaneda. For days, I equivocate about what to take and what to leave behind, until I reach the perfect balance of practicality and paranoia.

As I load the last milk jug of water into the car, Mrs. Atkins stares at me from the porch next door, nursing a sour look and a forty ounce of malt liquor. "You gonna mow that lawn before you head out?" she commands as much as asks. I bristle. "Paid someone to do it while I'm gone. He's supposed to be here today or the next at the latest." I am lying. My shaggy, seedy lawn is a hex sign designed to ward off the prying eyes of women who, like her, have appointed themselves my moral guardians. With a last fond look at my crabgrass and dandelions, I drive off.

Cruising down the quiet highways of weekday West Virginia, I play startling, incongruous music. The Violent Femmes query "Why can't I get just one fuck?" as the gentle hills roll by. Patti Smith rambles on in an endless stream of psychobabble as I pass by cows peacefully chewing their cud. I drive too fast, smoke too much, and play the music too loud in the hopes that I will frighten off the evil spirits that follow me, waiting for the moment of silence so they can whisper, in the voices of a thousand other people's mothers, that it is unsafe for a woman to go alone into the woods.

I park the car and follow the power lines up the mountain to my campsite. It seems that no one ever camps here but me; there is no sign of a fire pit or tamped earth. I set up my tent, which is advertised to go up in under five minutes but always takes me at least fifteen and then string a tarp up next to it. I unroll my sleeping bag and lash my pack to a tree to keep my food safe from scavengers. I gather rocks for a fire circle and set off to find wood.

The sun is beginning to set as I drag the last of the night's firewood into camp. I walk out to the edge of the rocky finger. Brilliant reds and pinks begin to touch the clouds that roll by beneath me. Like fire, the color creeps slowly toward me until I am standing in the sunset itself and then subsides, leaving the earth blackened with night. I stand for a moment, watching the stars come out. When the darkness is complete, I head back to camp to recreate the colors in my fire pit.

I lie down and wait for sleep. Sounds are magnified to my ears so used to the constant cacophony of cars and conversation. A chipmunk runs by and I hear a deer; a twig snaps and it is a bear. My dreams, when I sleep, are of vague dangers lurking just beyond the fire's light. I have come for solitude, but the woods seem full of claws and eyes. "What big teeth you have," I say to the night as I start awake again. All the better to eat you with, it replies.

The first trip I made alone to Beauty Mountain was in 1985. I was nineteen, and very much taken with the works of Baba Ram Dass and Carlos Castaneda. To prepare, I packed worn copies of Don Juan and *Be Here, Be Now, Be Nowhere*, but little else. I had not yet learned the value of dry socks or waterproof matches. Nature, I believed, was a kind mother who would welcome me to her bosom and nurture me in my quest for transformation. Surely, I would return from the mount an enlightened being, bathed in the golden glow of holiness that adorns the faces of Italian Gothic art.

That trip was nothing but conceit. I made plans less than I fantasized Disney-esque nature scenes complete with The Pastoral playing in the background. I chose my clothes not for warmth or durability, but for their value as costume. When I arrived at the site I gathered wood, built the fire ring, brewed tea, and pitched my tent as though I was playing to a full house on opening night. I recreated the actions even as I performed them, living the fiction I would later tell in embellished detail over beers at The Monarch.

I kept up the charade admirably during the daylight hours. The self I had constructed was efficient, competent and, most importantly, not afraid. For a few precious hours it seemed that all that was necessary for transformation was good character development. An act of such magnitude requires an audience, however, and by nightfall the façade began to crumble.

There I was, out in the middle of nowhere, by myself. The voices caught up with me. If you break your leg, don't come running to me, they said. Did they ever catch that guy who was killing girls along the Appalachian Trail? That Einstein girl never did have any sense. Catastrophic possibilities flashed before my eyes. I was paralyzed. I spent the rest of the night watching my possible deaths in the firelight. At dawn I crawled exhausted and defeated into my tent. That evening I drove home.

This year, as the darkness descends and the movie begins to play, I sit back and watch. I no longer come to this place in search of a holy vision, at least not in the same sense. I come here, year after year, to watch the film in my head play itself out.

Throughout the year, I am miserly with my fears. I put them in boxes labeled "fragile" and stuff them into cramped cupboards in the back of my mind. I wrap them like glass Christmas ornaments in newspaper clippings of men gone mad and women slain. I resist the urge to take them out and look at them, lest they shatter in my hand and leave me cut. And yet, if I leave them there unexamined and collecting dust, they begin to write gothic novels in the margins of my thoughts. And so, each year, I bring them here to hang them on the boughs of the hemlocks that surround this spot.

The fears have created for themselves a sort of hierarchy—the oldest and most organic have their turn first. As the sun disappears a nameless, annihilating dread comes over me. From early childhood, daughters are taught not to venture alone into the wood at night. Cautionary tales like "The Girl Who Trod on a Loaf" and "Little Red Riding Hood" fill our minds with grim images of agents of divine retribution lurking in the forest, waiting for us to step off the path. Only slightly less abstract warnings about "bad men" and original sin confirm our sense of being alien in the male world of the night wood. Even now, when the fear of anthropomorphized wolves seeking sexual favors and cakes baked for Granny is only an echo remembered from a more gullible time, the taste and timbre of the fear is the same. After all, the defense attorney would say, what was she doing out there alone at night anyway? And if she wasn't asking for it, why was she prancing around in that red cloak?

These old, childish fears quickly play themselves out. They are only the cartoons before the feature. There is a brief respite as the projectionist changes reels; in the past I have tricked myself into believing the movie is over. Now I know to use these few minutes of calm to feed the fire and put on more water for tea; the long haul is just beginning. I make a brew of valerian and lobelia, toss a bundle of sage into the fire, and settle in to see what horrors I have been collecting.

This year, the fire itself sparks the beginning of the movie, as pictures of riots flash before my eyes. Again, I see a trucker pulled from his cab and beaten by boys filled with rage. A familiar face rises up, bloodied and bruised, until a foot in a black, black boot shoves it down again. It is replaced by the bloodless face of my best friend's mother in her coffin. I had driven my friend down to the funeral, and then later to the trial, where her father was allowed to bargain down to manslaughter and do no prison time. I see a boy–naked, bleeding, scared–as he is handed over by police to his supposed lover. This year there has been a bumper crop of horrors, and I see them all again as I stare into the fire.

As the gray glow of dawn begins, the credits roll. I assign blame to make sense. Produced by the federal government, directed by the legal system, special effects by CNN … I pull radicalism around my shoulders like a protective blanket and crawl into my tent.

I spend my days with the routine terrors of copperheads and the ticks that invariably imbed themselves into my scalp. These minor, manageable villains help me to regain my sense of control.

I watch a group of rafts shoot through "Double Z"–an especially tricky set of rapids–but the screams of fear and delight are lost in the distance. Pink and purple mountain laurel surrounds me in a Georgia O'Keeffe fantasy; I find a stand of hemlock and lay down on the mossy ground. I feel self-indulgent and foolish for having been so frightened the night before.

I walk down the path to The Playhouse, a natural amphitheater that leads to a shelf overlooking the river. I play Portia and Gwendolen Fairfax to the trees. One should always have something fascinating to read on the train. By day, solitude grants amnesty from the seriousness of my burgeoning adulthood. I twirl and bow and ham it up, enjoying the sound of my own voice. And yet, as the first pinkness touches the clouds, I head back to my tent to prepare for the night's show.

The second night is more personal, the fears more familiar and thus less urgent. I imagine that I have left the coffee pot on and that my house is going up in flames. It occurs to me that if my father had a heart attack no one would be able to notify me. I worry that if something awful did happen to me up here, no one would think to go through my drawers and throw away the more embarrassing evidence before my mother got there. Is the neighbor's kid really feeding the cat? Maybe I shouldn't have paid him till I got back. By eleven, I crawl into my sleeping bag and fall asleep almost immediately.

In the morning I drive to a nearby town. After a truck-stop breakfast, I head down to Mermaid Rocks, a shallow place in the river where the hollows in the bedrock form natural Jacuzzis. I slip naked into the water. It pounds out the knots in my shoulders and kneads my back. I move to a deep pool and swim in aimless circles, searching out the warm spots. Driving away from the sunset and back to the mountain, I sing "Big Yellow Taxi" along with Joni Mitchell and wish I'd brought a bottle of wine.

The nights pass in peace now. I sit by the fire making plans rather than conjuring demons. I remodel my house a hundred times, adding turrets and gables and greenhouse windows. I create plot summaries for enough novels to last a lifetime and pretend to believe that I will write each one. I play aimless tunes on my penny whistle, weave vines into crude baskets, and miss my lover. Old friends stop by to visit, to talk about things I thought I had long forgotten. By day, I walk through the hollows and along the creek beds, remembering what keeps me in West Virginia. On my last night on the mountain a Bobwhite calls his own name as the sun goes down. Sar-ah, Sar-ah, Sar-ah, I answer him, recreating myself–sane, adult, brave–for the journey home.

George Winston plays quietly in the background as I drive back to Morgantown. My snakebite kit and rain poncho lay blessedly unused in the bottom of my pack and there are still three full jugs of water in the trunk. I am only mildly disturbed by the metallic naked women on the mud flaps of the truck that plays leapfrog with me between Big Otter and Flatwoods. Having just burned up a year's worth of psychic garbage at my campfire, I can afford to be a little forgiving.

As I pull up in front of my house, I see that the yard has

turned from bush to jungle in my absence and that the mail sits uncollected in a stack beneath the mailbox. The cat eyes me reproachfully as I unlock the door, and to punish me refuses the first can of food I open for her. The answering machine blinks, but I ignore it. The house fills with the smell of wood smoke and I realize I need a shower.

Hot water courses over my body, washing away the last of the sweat and the grit accumulated over the week. I pull on the silk nightshirt brought back from Paris as a consolation prize by an old lover and crawl between cool, clean sheets. I begin to reach for the Mary Daly I had been reading when I left, but my hand lights instead on the more familiar pleasures of Charlotte Bronte. It's too early to start collecting fears for next year's trip. As I settle in to help poor Jane navigate the treacherous road to womanhood, I make a mental note to borrow Mrs. Atkins' lawnmower in the morning and to call my mother and tell her that I survived.

The Way Things Go
1973

When I was eight years old, Dad came home with a Thing. It was the kind of thing, my mother made clear, that a grown man in his thirties, the father of three children for God's sake, should have had more sense than to buy. But, then again, this was just the sort of thing she had come to expect from him. She would warm to it eventually, but on that first day she was horrified. I, of course, loved my father's beautiful, transgressive Thing from the moment I saw it in the driveway. While it didn't hurt that Mom hated it as much as she hated messy rooms and sass-mouth, I would have loved it for its Sunshine Yellow paint alone.

The Volkswagen Thing was a cult hit. Half car, half erector set, it was the epitome of the big boy toy. My younger brothers and I watched in awe as Dad took the doors and windows off, put the windshield down, stowed the ragtop, and folded the back seat into the floor. Voila–it looked just like a dune buggy! Click the whole thing back together, and it was almost a Jeep. Dad still hadn't lost his college linebacker bulk and when he squeezed behind the wheel of the Thing, it looked more like an oversized Tonka truck than a real car.

Originally created as a military vehicle for the German army in World War II, it was hard to imagine Nazi soldiers driving around in these surfer-mobiles. Sold in this country in Sunshine Yellow, Blizzard White, and Pumpkin Orange, they just seemed too silly to be war machines. And Things had some serious flaws. At speeds over 40, the plastic windows pulled away from the top, letting in rain and road dust. Their top speed was 68 mph, and if you pushed them to it, they would shimmy and shake like Sandra Dee in *Gidget Goes Hawaiian*. Their primary virtue was their simplicity; they had engines not much more complicated than the ones in lawn mowers and bodies made of sheet metal. They were like the paintings of de Kooning or the music of Yma Sumac – you either "got it" or you didn't. If you got it, it made you feel better about yourself that you did. If you didn't, you felt smugly certain that there wasn't really anything to get.

In 1980, Volkswagen stopped production of the Thing. By then, Dad had long since sold his and was driving my dead grandfather's silver Lincoln Town Car. It was, as I remember, his first real sacrifice to the realities of middle age.

2002

Life since the Thing has not been kind to Dad. His career failed when the bottom dropped out of the coal market. His marriage to my mother dissolved shortly thereafter and a rough decade or so followed. It was a time when there wasn't much any of us could do but sit back and hope he'd find his way to happier times. It wasn't until well into his fifty-ninth year that we started to think maybe he had.

As Dad's sixtieth birthday approached, it became more and more important to me to find a meaningful way to mark it. A party was out. It would have required too much agreement, a level of cooperation that my siblings and I just couldn't pull off. Haven, my younger sister with whom Dad is permanently houseguesting, suggested that we send him on a year-long eco-tourism tour she had seen advertised somewhere. Unfortunately, our combined savings weren't up to anything so grand. I was afraid I was going to have to fall back on the old standby: a shirt from L.L. Bean that he would put, still wrapped, in the closet where he kept all the other unopened gifts we'd given him over the years. Dad says there is nothing he needs; in reality, he's just too contrary to risk actually liking any of our gifts. Pleased isn't in his emotional repertoire.

Three weeks before the big day, and still without a plan, I got an email from Dad with a link to an auction on Ebay that read simply, "I don't know how to use Ebay. If you'll buy this and help me pick it up, I'll pay for it." Before I could even open the link, my screen flashed with an instant message from my sister: "DO NOT BUY THAT THING FOR DAD OR I WILL KILL YOU WITH MY BARE HANDS!" Whatever Dad wanted, Haven had already told him he couldn't have it. I didn't like her casual reversing of their roles. It suggested that Dad was not just a guy who needed a little time and support to get back on his feet; it suggested a decline I did not think had yet begun.

I clicked on the link and laughed. Dad wasn't asking for help to buy something, he was asking for help to buy some Thing. It was battered, but the ad said it ran, and it was cheap. It belonged to a young engineer in Huntsville, Alabama, the home of Putt, one of my best and oldest friends. Before I could finish reading the listing, a second instant message popped up. "IF YOU BUY IT FOR HIM, HE'S MOVING IN WITH YOU. I AM *NOT* KIDDING!" Dad, reading over her shoulder, called immediately, said simply "Yes she is. She's been raised better than that," and hung up. Obviously Haven, who was too young to remember Dad's first Thing, was one of those people who didn't get their charm. At least, didn't get it enough to want one up on blocks in her front yard. I responded, "C'mon, don't you think he should have whatever he wants for his sixtieth birthday?" She shot back, without a second's hesitation, "NOPE."

  I love my sister, but nothing could have ensured I would help Dad buy and bring home the Thing as surely as her disapproval. It was a chance to be on the wrong side of things with my father once again, the first chance in a long time to share with him the smugness that comes from being the only ones in the room who get the joke. Haven tried her best to dissuade me. She threatened, she begged, she even emailed my home phone number to the sixteen year old girl I was bidding against so she could call to try to play on my sympathies. I apologized to ILUVAJMcLean when she called, and I meant it, but as I was talking to her I put in a bid I knew she couldn't match and the Thing was ours.

A few weeks later, we loaded up my Chevy Lumina–a car that is to the Thing what Perry Como is to The Grateful Dead–and headed for Dixie. It was a beautiful June Saturday; we had a tank of gas, two pairs of cheap sunglasses, a cooler of chocolate milk and Diet Pepsi, and fourteen hours for an easy eight-hour drive. Our mood was decidedly festive as we cruised down Highway 64, passing the Kentucky countryside at about 85.

It was idyllic for, oh, probably all of forty-five minutes. I'd forgotten one of the primary rules for car trips with Dad–don't let him listen to the news. I don't believe my father has deeply held political convictions. His opinions are completely situational–he pretends to believe whatever will most annoy the people around him at the moment. That morning a puff piece on NPR about the opening of the National Cowgirl Museum and Hall of Fame sparked a heated debate about what he quaintly refers to as "women's lib." It was political farce, with Dad playing the part of the Southern Gentleman Bigot. Born in Virginia, he likes to pepper his speech with stories about Mr. Jefferson and The University, y'alls and a put on twang. I think this act is a parody of his father, who never could be taught to stop using words like "colored," "darkie" and my personal favorite, "kike." It's improbable, but while I get my obviously Jewish last name from my father, I am Jewish and he is not.

I don't remember how the argument that morning was resolved, or even if it was. I do remember, though, having some serious second thoughts about our plans to meet Putt and her girlfriend Shawna for dinner. If he could riff for half an hour on the sheer wrongness of honoring cowgirls with their own museum, I didn't want to think about how much fun he was likely to be over dinner with a couple of lesbians.

Kentucky rolled by greenly and uneventfully. On the far side of Lexington, Dad popped Janis Joplin's *Pearl* into the tape deck and, with the windows rolled down, we sang along all the way to Bardstown. A guy in a pick-up truck kept pace just long enough to join us in the lines, "from the Kentucky coal mines/ to the California sun/ Bobby shared the secrets of my soul," whoop, and speed off. For a ten mile stretch of road, Dad was the dramatic victim in a series of drive-by shootings executed by a six-year-old with a plastic rifle. Every fifteen minutes or so, he remembered to whine, "Are we there yet? I'm bored!" Outside Campbellsville, Dad changed his complaint to, "I need to go to the bathroom"; it wasn't until we were almost to Bowling Green that I realized he wasn't kidding.

We stopped for a bathroom break and a quick lunch at a Dairy Queen outside Cave City. Waxing nostalgic, Dad told an old story about his first job, at a Dairy Queen. He worked there until a woman, having just ordered and received three strawberry milkshakes, cocked her head and asked, "Could you make one of those chocolate instead?" "Let me see," he'd said, waggling his fingers and muttering incantations. Lifting the lid of one, he turned to the woman with a look of great disappointment. "Nope, it's still strawberry." Neither the lady, nor his boss, found this funny. "That's the problem with people," Dad opined, "they just don't get it." He remembers his life this way, through a rosary of oft-told stories, and these stories are all I know of who he has been other than my father. What I like about them is that they leave out the rough spots; they tell a larger story of a life it wouldn't be so bad to have lived.

Back on the road, Dad drifted off, snoring quietly in the seat next to me as I drove the sunny highway across the border into Tennessee. Once I was certain he was asleep, I tossed Janis and popped in an old War cassette I'd picked up at a garage sale the week before. *All my friends know the low rider* ... Music made for the road, music that sounds silly played in an apartment or a bar. While Dad napped, I rocked out down Highway 65. Further into Tennessee, the car to truck ratio tipped in favor of trucks, and the prevalence of yellow ribbon decals made the highway look like a field of spring daffodils. Toward Nashville, the billboards hawked tourist traps, banks, and country music stations. Further south, roadside signs advertised salvation and some place called "The Boobie Bungalow." *Take a little trip, take a little trip, take a little trip with me...*

Just past Lynnville, I noticed my Lumina didn't seem to have as much pick-up as before. And it looked to me as if the clock was dimmer, seemed as if the music was quieter than it had been only a moment ago. I turned off the air-conditioning and that helped, but only for about twenty miles. I watched in dismay as the speedometer fell below forty and stayed there. Finally, outside Pulaski, I had no choice but to pull over. Dad got out, looked under the hood, and said it was probably the alternator but who could tell with all the damned computer equipment cluttering up the engine? We sat by the side of the road, drinking the last of the Diet Pepsi and soaking bandanas in the icy water in the bottom of the cooler to wrap around our necks, waiting for AAA to send someone.

Pulaski, Tennessee has the sad distinction of being the birthplace of the Ku Klux Klan. The folks I know from around there say the town has worked hard to live down its history. Apparently, though, no one had told our tow truck driver that things had changed in Pulaski, that they weren't doing ignorant redneck in Tennessee anymore. He pulled up, got out, and asked to see my license. "Einstein?" he said questioningly. I nodded; waiting for the inevitable "any relation?" so I could deliver my standard "Only the hair is genetic." That wasn't his question, though. Looking down at my West Virginia license he sniggered, "You all from Jew York?" I was dumbfounded, so he asked again, a little more forcefully this time. "I said, you guys from Jew York?"

There we were, one true and one false Jew, standing by the side of the highway in Tennessee, looking for an answer to the question of whether or not we were from Jew York. I waited for Dad to do what fathers do when their daughters are insulted, for him to say "Now, you look here, young man…" or maybe take a swing at the son of a bitch. I waited for him to flash some secret Southern sign that would clue this guy in to the cracker side of my heritage. I turned to Dad expectantly and saw for the first time the deep lines on his face, the fragile bones of his wrists on thin arms, the tired slump of his shoulders. "No," I answered quickly, "we're from West Virginia," as if the question had been that question all along.

I sat uncomfortably between the tow truck driver and Dad for the twenty-minute ride back to his garage–the only garage, he informed us, still open at the very late hour of 2pm on a Saturday. I wanted to joke; to point out that everything in New York shuts down on Saturday, too; to say *Shabbat Shalom*. Instead, I sat in silence as he listed all the reasons this was going to cost me big. Since it was a Saturday afternoon, he was going to have to charge me double for the labor. He was going to have to drive to a neighboring town for the part, so there would be that time and the mileage. And, even though officially AAA would pay for the tow up to a hundred miles, the last twelve miles weren't highway miles, so of course he was going have to charge me two and a half dollars a mile for those, too. "'Course," he said, "I guess an extra couple hundred dollars don't mean much to folks like you."

Folks like us? We were both wearing jeans with frayed cuffs and battered old t-shirts. My only jewelry was an irregularly shaped rock tied with a leather lanyard around my neck–a gift from one of my favorite three year olds–beautiful to me but hardly ostentatious. Hadn't this guy just loaded my dinged up, broken down, ten-year-old car onto the back of his tow truck? However clever he was at identifying ethnicity, he was a lousy judge of net worth.

In the end, though, it didn't matter whether or not the money was easy or hard for me to come by; I had to pay what he asked. He left Dad and me on the porch of his shop and headed off to fetch the part he needed. We drank fruit-flavored sodas from the vending machine while I fed Dad the straight lines that elicited the best of his stories: the one about getting busted for performing a black mass in the monk's graveyard when he was a freshman at Belmont Abbey; the time, changing my diaper, he knocked off the stump of my umbilical cord and sobbed for three hours behind a locked bathroom door. Stories about how he rescued his knuckle-headed first born from cold-hearted gym teachers, ne'er-do-well boyfriends, and the attack parrots which seemed to follow us from family vacation to family vacation when I was a child. The telling put things back to right: Dad the protector, me the hapless kid always getting into trouble.

The tow truck driver came back after about an hour, smelling of beer and carrying the world's only two hundred fifty dollar rebuilt alternator. While he tinkered with the car, I called Putt to tell her we were running late, "We're in Pulaski." She sounded genuinely concerned. "Do you need me to come up there and get y'all?" It took several minutes to dissuade her. "Well, as long as your daddy's with you, I guess you'll be okay, but for God's sake be careful and keep your mouth shut." By the end of it, the bill was four hundred and eighty five dollars. As we pulled away, I rolled down my window, smiled, and called out cheerily, *Geh cocken offen yom, Putznasher!* He smiled back and waved, fanning out the wad of bills in his hand for me to see.

	Safely back on Interstate 65, we continued on as if nothing unusual had happened, and maybe it hadn't. "We got screwed," Dad mused, laughing and lighting a cigarette, "but we didn't get lynched. I guess things have changed around here."

The state of Alabama is littered with military equipment displayed as trophies or used as playground equipment. In light of the day we'd had, these cast-off Blackhawk helicopters and M42 Dusters looked like thinly veiled threats to me; they put some muscle behind the oft-repeated The-South-Will-Rise-Again sloganeering of the country music station we'd been listening to since Pulaski. The exit we wanted was marked by a Saturn V Rocket; a tribute to Werner von Braun, the city's favorite adopted son.

	Huntsville is an ugly, sprawling city of low buildings and pragmatic architecture inhabited by engineers and soldiers. Putt had, for years, worked at Redstone Arsenal in Aviation and

Missile Research on projects she hinted were top secret. She'd recently given it all up, finally realized that developing missile guidance systems was the wrong career for an ethical vegetarian peacenik and started her own handywoman business.

We met Putt and Shawna at The Greenbrier Restaurant, a catfish and barbeque joint that is a legend among road food aficionados. Over huge plates of pork shoulder, cornmeal-encrusted catfish, slaw, pickles, and potatoes, Dad, Putt, and Shawna spoke in the arcane language of engineers about the viability of fuel cell technology and how to build a butter churn from a cement mixer. I noticed Shawna wipe a smear of barbeque sauce from Putt's cheek with her napkin and later, over the inevitable pie that ends Southern suppers, drape her arm around Putt's shoulder. Dad didn't flinch, nor did the seven or eight local families seated around the identical Formica tables on all sides of us.

The elaborate rules that govern how Southerners interact have always been opaque to me. I was once married to a man who had grown up in Birmingham, right next door to Bull Connor. Though by no means supporters of Connor's reactionary politics or his famously brutal methods, my husband and his family had still done all the neighborly things people do: brought in the mail when the Connors traveled, baked them fruitcakes at Christmas, invited them to neighborhood cook-outs. While the nation watched Bull Connor turn fire hoses and attack dogs on unarmed demonstrators, my future in-laws smiled and waved a neighborly "Hello" to him when passing on the street. Anything else would have been rude, my former mother-in-law once told me. My ex-husband and I fought about this throughout our marriage; he staunchly insisted that there is never anything wrong with being polite, and I never stopped believing he had shirked his moral obligation to throw bricks through the Connors' windows every morning on his way to school.

Sitting in The Greenbrier eating pie with Putt and Shawna, I could have believed that things had changed radically down South in the intervening years. It would have been easy on any other day. When Putt rested her hand on Shawna's knee as the plates were cleared away, it was an act of simple affection, not of defiance. Men with WWJD on their baseball caps and NASCAR belt buckles did not bother to stop chewing long enough to give it a second thought, although they sat only a few feet away and could not help but see. Their tolerance had something to do with the fact that Putt and Shawna were from "around here"–not this town, but from towns as deeply Southern–and something to do with the fact that they, themselves, were comfortable and the affections between them were of the small, unconscious sort that become the habits of love over time. Later, Putt and I would agree that the whole place might have erupted in a riot had they kissed, but we would also recall the times twenty years before–when it had been her arm around my shoulder–that we had been asked to leave more than one place for less.

By eight the next morning Dad and I were driving through a subdivision made up entirely of identical duplexes, trying to figure out a numbering system that seemed either random or based on an incredibly complicated algorithm. In Huntsville, it didn't seem impossible that the non-sequential numbers added up to a very funny mathematical joke but if they did, we never got it. We drove around until we spotted a guy in a t-shirt that read "Byte Me" standing in front of a battered, topless Thing. At a distance, it looked like he'd painted it camo; on closer inspection, it was a dark green with lots of rust and Bondo. He showed Dad the engine, explained a few of the Thing's quirks, and gave him a screwdriver in case the gas pedal stuck, as it sometimes did. Dad gave him fifteen hundred dollars and, at the guy's request, took a last picture of him with the Thing before he signed over the title.

Originally, the plan had been to tow the Thing back to West Virginia, but in the end Dad had managed to arrange things so that he would have to drive it the four hundred and fifty miles while I followed in case he broke down. Popping the trunk, he showed me the tiny engine. "The only thing that can break is the belt, and if that goes, you can fix it with a nylon stocking."

The trip back was surprisingly uneventful. The Thing managed to cruise along quite nicely at sixty miles an hour for an hour, an hour and a half, at a stretch. When it had had enough, it would die slowly, giving Dad just enough time to pull over onto the shoulder. We'd sit there, smoking and waiting for the engine to cool down, watching the trucks and cars go by. In my pocket, I had the number of a towing company in Pulaski Putt said could be trusted–just in case–but the Thing always started up again.

By the time we passed Nashville, the sky had turned cloudy. We crossed the Kentucky border in the first of three cloudbursts, the rain pounding down hard on Dad as he drove. I honked and flashed my lights, but he just waved happily from up ahead. When he did have to pull over again to let the engine cool down, he pointed to the holes in the floor and said proudly, "See? Water runs right out of it. It'll take more than a little rainstorm to keep my Thing and me off the road!" With his hair frizzed into a gray afro and the wrinkles around his eyes and mouth outlined in road grime, he still somehow looked more like the father of my childhood than he had in a very long time.

It was just getting dark as we crossed back into West Virginia. Dad waved one last time as he pulled off at the exit for Huntington. I rolled down my window to wave back and caught him singing loudly to himself, "I'm a man of means by no means/ King of the Road!" Laughing, I drove away. I had three more hours to go until I made it home to Morgantown. I was tired, but it seemed safer not to risk Haven's hospitality.

2006

The Thing has been retired to a rented garage and months go by without Dad checking on it. It took a year, but Haven finally got him to move it out of her front yard. By then, the seats had been discarded as unsalvageable, and he had to duct tape a plastic lawn chair to the floor in order to drive it to the storage lot. Cars and trucks honked as he chugged along Alternate Route 10, unable to go over 25 without being shaken out. Haven was humiliated, but I believe the honks were ones of encouragement, not annoyance. If he'd had two lawn chairs, I would have happily ridden beside him. But being Dad, he only had one.

He's had offers to sell it for a nice profit. When he doesn't take them, Haven shakes her head and talks about how much it costs him a month to keep it in storage. Dad calls so that we can cluck our tongues at Haven for not getting it. She calls to remind me that it's a lot funnier from three hours away, that she'll never understand why he keeps an old car that can't be driven, and to point out that he could use that money to get an apartment of his own. "I guess that's just the way things go," she says, "or, in this case, don't go." It's getting to be an old joke, but we laugh anyway. These are happier times.

Almost Home

Late on my first day out of the fallout shelter, I wander into Flatwoods, West Virginia. I can hear weapons fire in the distance, and footsteps, both of which make me wary, but the message that was left for me outside the fallout shelter said to head here to get help, and I sure could use some help. I've already died once, and although I've found a gun, I am a lousy shot. I crouch low, trying to stay hidden, and crab-walk through the rubble around the main street. The last time I was here, it was to buy one-dollar seconds at the Fiesta Ware outlet and old-fashioned candies at the faux-Amish bulk foods store on the outskirts of town. Before they built the outlet mall, the only reason people stopped was to gas up on their way to somewhere else; it's always been that sort of town. Now, the mall is gone, as are most of the gas stations and all of the people. This Flatwoods is populated only by other survivors, malfunctioning robots, and zombie-esque creatures we call "the Scorched."

I'm in Bethesda Game Studio's *Fallout 76*, a survival game that marks the venerable franchise's first move into multiplayer, online world-building. The year is 2102, and it's twenty-five years after a devastating nuclear war. I've just been let out of Vault 76, a fallout shelter meant to house the best and the brightest, situated in rural West Virginia. In theory, it's our job as players to rebuild the world, but we don't have enough control over the narrative to do that. We can't form governments or undertake large-scale environmental projects, and nothing we do in the game impacts the overall story arc. Instead of rebuilding, our characters kill the monsters, loot their bodies, build better weapons, then kill the monsters again.

This really isn't my sort of game; I love computer games, but I usually play the ones called *massively multiplayer online role-playing games* (MMORPGs) with elves and magic and simple targeting systems so that you don't actually have to be good at them unless you want to take on the biggest of the bads. It's the story that draws the player through such games; the best of them are akin to interactive novels full of rich narrative and potential for character development. *Fallout 76* is fundamentally a first-person shooter game, and it requires skills and a certain bloodlust that I lack. There isn't, at least at launch, much of a narrative. Instead, it's what's called a *sandbox game*, meaning that the player can go anywhere and do anything, and there is no narrative thread that must be followed. It's the kind of game players want to be good at instead of the kind of game they want to immerse themselves in. I will never be good at it. No matter how I try, I can't seem to hit anything with my shotgun, though in real life I used to be a passable skeet shooter. Slashing at things with my machete seems to work all right, but it's mostly blind flailing, and if it were possible, I'd probably hack myself to death before I killed my prey.

I'm playing because I love this place. I grew up here and come back often. When my life goes to ground, as it has a few times, I return to West Virginia to get back on my feet. It's home. The opportunity to go back there—to dip in and out of nostalgia any time I like—is just too lovely to pass up.

In this future Flatwoods, as in reality, the houses look akin to the house I lived in for a while in Morgantown, which the realtor called "a vernacular farmhouse with Victorian pretensions." Clapboard exteriors with peeling white or pastel paint, concrete steps leading up to sagging porches, pathways to the back doors because in Appalachia, friends and family come in through the back and only the law and the mailman come to the front. I love that the game developers got this detail right.

There is a trailer or two, a diner, a gas station, and an old church repurposed as an infirmary and trading post, where I find the Overseer's next note to me and directions to head to Morgantown. This is a West Virginia whose aesthetic is frozen in the era of mid-century modern furniture and true rurality, before Walmart and Dollar General rebuilt every kind of American poverty out of extruded plastic. I am wearing a faded blue dress that's more *The Waltons* than *The Jetsons*. Other players clump around in heavy robotic armor or wear discarded amusement park uniforms. The yards are littered with the detritus of life before the war: dirty ashtrays, empty beer bottles, pipe wrenches, and farming tools. Some of the other leavings are heartbreaking. I find teddy bears and abandoned wheelchairs, empty cribs and notes about running out on errands from which the note writers never returned. I pick up abandoned chessboards, burnt magazines, and cans of dog food. There are bodies everywhere. I pick up bones and put them in my rucksack. Everything is scarce, and so nothing useful can be allowed to molder into nothingness. This, too, feels very Appalachian to me.

I pick up as much as I can carry, to scrap later and turn into guns, bullets, and armor that I will wear under my dress. I sell the few valuables to the robot who mans the trading station. He says the Overseer—and I'm not yet certain who, really, that is—has told him to expect more humans and that it's good to see us. I'm reminded of the Tin Man, standing alone in a patch of woods until Dorothy happens by. The melancholia this inspires in me feels genuine.

I build myself a small camp on a nearby hill, set up a workshop to repair my kit and a kitchen to brew teas and roast wild game. I'm not from the sort of West Virginia family that goes deer hunting, but it's clear that if I'm going to survive, I'm going to have to hunt for my own food and protect myself from the Scorched, so I spend the first several days stalking mutated steers and two-headed deer called *radstags* and teaching myself the game's mechanics: how to shoot, how to travel, how to build. There are possums, but I don't kill them because I've had possum once and don't want even to pretend to eat it again. I cook up venison steaks and vegetable stews at my camp and pass the food out to newcomers because I make a lot more than I can carry and the game forces players to eat and stay hydrated. Except for the interactions with other players, it's the boring part of the game.

I also start to find survivor stories: brief narrated audio clips about the people whose camps and houses I'm plundering. I've been worried about this. West Virginia doesn't usually fare well when it's portrayed in pop culture, and I'm concerned that tropes about hillbillies will overwrite the joy of exploring the landscape. But these stories aren't that; they are lovely and varied and poignant. There is the story of the reverend who loses his faith, then finds it again, during the aftermath of the bombs. Of the junkie who steals food from this reverend and sets up camp across the river. Of the programmer for the company that built the vault, who falls in love amidst all the destruction. (Later, I will come to suspect that the young programmer has fallen in love with the junkie, as I begin to see the subtle ways their stories intertwine.) And on and on—a rich and varied tapestry of people, more *Spoon River Anthology* than *The Hills Have Eyes*.

There are parts of the game I find stressful instead of engrossing. I hate the need to keep up my guard, to kill things that the game developers insist are no longer human but which seem pretty human to me—what with their talking and shooting and having human-shaped bodies—though I understand the shooting is the reason most of the players are here. While I'm puttering around gathering soot flowers and bloodleaf plants to make healing salves, more serious players are racing around in heavy battle armor, strafing the landscape with machine gun fire, and occasionally setting off their own nuclear bombs.

The first time I venture toward Morgantown, I run into two heavily armored combatants who show up on my screen as Cocktimus Prime and Screaming Semen. They shoot at me once, but after I assure them I'm just passing through and mean them no harm, they put down their guns.

There are two ways to communicate in the game: via a few built-in emotes such as *wave* or *trade*, or by speaking into the game world through a microphone. I prefer the latter, which means that when I tell Cocktimus and Screaming, whom I cannot help but imagine are teenage boys, that I mean them no harm, they hear me as I am. I put a little extra "mom voice" into it and say, "But really? Those are the names you've chosen for yourselves?" and they fast-travel away.

One might imagine that I'm the interloper here, that middle-aged ladies are rare in these virtual worlds, but that's not true. According to the Entertainment Software Association, an industry group that tracks trends in video gaming, adult women made up a substantially larger portion of the 2018 gaming population (33 percent) than boys under eighteen (17 percent), and the average woman who played video games that year was thirty-six years old. In fact, the next person I meet is a woman who plays with her husband, and although I don't know her age, she is clearly more adult than not. She offers me things that would make the game easier: a better gun, some new armor, some grenades. I say thank you but no; I like that it's slow going.

Asheron's Call was one of the first of this sort of game, and the first I played. When it launched in 1999, I was in my mid-thirties, living in a studio apartment in Manhattan and working sixty- to seventy-hour weeks at an advertising agency as an interactive marketing specialist. I'd aged out of going to clubs on weeknights, and most of the people I knew commuted out of the city, and back to families, at the end of the workday. I was dating someone, but only in a dinner-on-Friday-nights kind of way. I was bored and lonely during the week.

It seems silly now, but there was something wondrous about the game on the day it launched. One minute, I was sitting at my desk in a living room roughly the size of a walk-in closet, and the next, I was in a wooded area surrounded by confused mages and warriors, all milling about and asking one another how to do the simplest thing, such as pick up a stick or don a shirt. This sort of game was new enough that most of the people who'd signed in had never been in a multiplayer game environment before, and the sort of posturing that would later become a hallmark of online gaming was entirely absent. We were, to borrow from the language that would develop as shared gaming became more popular, all *n00bs*.

The story that drove the game was complex, dynamic, and entirely beside the point—except for the way it forced interaction with other players. Early on, I met a crusty old war mage named Lerrick, and we'd sit in the taverns that dotted the landscape and argue about meta-gaming issues. Were we liberators or colonizers in this world? Was it ethical that we were sometimes called on to kill the children of our enemies? We'd hash all this out over pretend tankards of ale while digital battles raged outside. Later, I met a young warrior who gifted me with powerful armor and weapons, and we would venture into monster dens and ancient citadels together. It was courtship, of a sort, and although he told me his name, I don't know if he lied. I certainly did. I think I told him my name was Cathy, but it might have been Cindy or Kate. I don't remember now.

The game ran on until 2017, though I'd stopped playing within six months and never played often or well enough to have a high-level character. After a time, the underlying processes of games become too apparent to me. I can see the data modeling behind the quests to kill six rats, fetch ten of some particular herb, travel to a certain place to speak to a specific person. And when that happens, it stops being compelling, the illusion falls away, and it might be years before I pick up a new game out of curiosity about how the medium has evolved.

The interesting part of *Fallout 76* is getting to explore recreations of spaces I know intimately. My hometown isn't in the game, but the amusement park that hosted every Safety Patrol and Campfire Girl outing of my childhood is. There are exact replicas of an old wooden roller coaster that never looked any safer in real life than it does in the game, and the bumper cars that I rode on one of my first dates. A little to the north is the hot dog restaurant that I visit with my family on trips home; to the west, an abandoned mountain top removal site that has played a significant and complicated role in my family's history. In Morgantown, I can stand in the very classroom where I took a class from Kevin Oderman on the poetry of H.D., and I can sit in the bar where my first husband and I signed our divorce papers over bottles of beer. The tension between the nostalgic setting and the horrors of the post-apocalyptic setting is oddly pleasant. Maybe it's because the Appalachia of my childhood was always already half-ruined; the empty department stores and torn-up roads don't seem unusual.

But here, in this simulacrum, the game offers a chance to recreate West Virginia as more u- than dys-topia. That's what all of these games offer: the illusion of a world in which we, as the players, have the ability to fix what's wrong. As gamer and games journalist Keith Stuart writes for the *Guardian*, "Games are about shared experiences, rendered extraordinarily powerful by interaction and ownership." There are monsters to battle, rights to wrong, survivors to aid, and, so, amid the rubble is also the promise of better days. There may be little that I, as an individual, can do to stop climate change or mass shootings in the real world, but in a game world, I am powerful and can right most of the wrongs. After a few weeks of play, I have armor that makes me nearly invulnerable and weapons strong enough that I can kill waves of mutants in minutes. They've quickly become a nuisance rather than a threat, and once I can move freely through the world, I'm able to start imagining better ways for it to be. This is a lesson in privilege, resources, and safety.

I use the tools of Appalachian activism, borrowing from back-to-the-land and arts organizations like Appalshop: people want to create. I build a farmer's market on the outskirts of Flatwoods, where I host twice-weekly poetry readings, tall-tale-telling contests, and open mic comedy. At first, I imagine nobody will come, but there is a steady stream of people, and then that steady stream turns into a group of regulars. They donate all the game's best items—the most powerful weapons, the best armor, the rarest ingredients for medicines and drugs—for me to offer as prizes, but in truth, they're the only ones who come and they don't need these things, so the items languish in my inventory until they become obsolete as the game developers release more powerful items into the world. After a while, everyone still gathers, but the poetry readings and tall-tale-telling contests have fewer and fewer participants. They've come for the camaraderie, but that isn't enough to hold them, so I begin to plan outings.

I use what I know of West Virginian history to give tours of landmarks in the game. The tours start with the old Trans-Allegheny Lunatic Asylum, a place whose long and horrific history I know well. Walking through the virtual hallways, I tell a group of ten about the history of lobotomies, labor exploitation, torture, and profiteering that marked not just this place but the entire asylum movement. They ask respectful questions. They are appropriately horrified and moved. Unlike the actual visitors on the last tour I attended in the real world, they don't suggest that things were better then or that surely it was never as bad as all that.

Soon, I am spending ten to twelve hours a week researching places whose histories I don't already know: the Krishna temple and the old prison in Moundsville; the nuclear bunker built for Congress in White Sulphur Springs; and the little town of Helvetia, which still clings to the folk traditions of the German and Swedish immigrants who settled it several generations ago. Not all of these tours go well. If I don't put in enough time researching a place beforehand, I do little more than regurgitate information anyone could find on Wikipedia. When I lapse into personal stories, the other players listen politely, but—surrounded as we are by the threats of mutants and monsters—the stories have little resonance or meaning.

Eventually, I give up the tours and the farmer's market. They require too much effort and mimic too closely the work I do to prepare to teach class in real life. The game not only stops being fun, but it stops being interesting to me. For a few months, I stop playing altogether.

Then, in a way that's not possible in the real world, I sneak back in as an entirely different person, with a new name and a new account. I avoid making friends, or playing with the friends I have already made, and I stay away from the difficult content that requires teams of players. I don't care about acquiring high-powered items or beating tough challenges. Instead, I walk along the creek beds and railroad tracks in the parts of the game where there are mostly just trees and mountains. It's a place I go when I need a short break from the work I am doing but don't have time to go walk in the Tennessee woods near where I live now. If I log in for two hours in any given week, that's a lot. I'm more likely to spend fifteen minutes every few days picking flowers and walking the streets of towns I know for moments of nostalgia.

This isn't the way the game was meant to be played, but maybe what I'm doing is something other than playing the game. The narrative through-line is now entirely opaque to me; I don't bother to keep up with the content updates that move the story along. I avoid the places where the map shows activity and stay away from other players' camps. When, by accident, I stumble across other people, I simply log out. This, too, is a special kind of joy: to just disappear when one's solitude is intruded upon.

Soon enough, the day will come when I uninstall the game—probably when the next game that's new and interesting enough to attract my attention launches and I need the disk space to run it. I will stay in that new world long enough to see its wonders and then be gone again. These virtual worlds can be fabulous places to tourist, but they are not anywhere that someone should try to build a life.

Shelter

The day I met Wilbur, the snow was coming down so hard and fast I had to walk to work. My battered old car and its bald tires couldn't be trusted on icy pavement, and already the drifts lay as high as the front bumper. I was scheduled for a double shift – 8 a.m. to midnight – at Bartlett House, a homeless shelter, and figured that even if I could get the car there, I'd have to leave it behind when it was time to go home. The weather report called for another foot of snow. So, bundled in my mother's hand-me-down parka, my roommate's too-big snow boots, and a scarf, I walked the few miles to the shelter through the beginnings of what would come to be known as The Great Blizzard of 1993.

Bartlett House served the homeless in Morgantown, West Virginia, and its surrounding areas. It was new then, with only a handful of dormitory rooms, a large communal area for watching television and eating meals, an industrial kitchen, and three offices. The shelter had a men's room and a women's room, each with two toilets and two showers, and another half bath behind the locked door of the general staff office. There were enough beds for forty people. By the time I got to work that morning, forty-seven had checked in for the day.

"The police are bringing everybody in," Rich told me. He had worked the overnight shift. "Not just the guys off the riverbank, either. I mean everybody." He gestured to the hallway packed with people, pointing to one guy in particular: Melvin. We'd kicked him out of the shelter a few months earlier when, after other residents had complained of a terrible smell coming from his bunk, we'd discovered several decomposing squirrel carcasses and a hunting knife tucked inside his rucksack. He'd refused to give up either, saying the food we served was full of poison and he preferred to eat what he could kill on his own. Even the police were wary of Melvin, who was rumored to now be living in a sewer pipe near the Walmart and subsisting on feral cats and roadkill.

"Did they take his knife away?" I asked.

"They said they did," Rich answered, in a way that suggested there was a good chance they hadn't.

"The cops said we couldn't turn anybody away until the weather breaks." Rich handed me the bed-assignment chart and the cordless phone, our link to outside help in an emergency. He said he had run out of blankets, so he'd been giving out the towels and extra mattress pads, but we were almost out of those, too. He also told me there was space left on the floors in a couple of rooms, but other than that, the shelter was full.

After Rich left, I gathered a small corps of long-term residents and, together, we worked out a strategy for dealing with the sudden influx of so many people. Traveling Jack and Cat-Eyes sat guard near the door and escorted the people who came in throughout the day back to the kitchen, where I wrote their names in the margins of the bed-assignment chart and showed them to a space on the floor where they could sleep. Rita and Star peeled fifty pounds of potatoes, Errol boiled them in batches, and Granny Lynn mashed them with commodity butter and tins of evaporated milk. Carthelius helped me pull pounds upon pounds of ground venison out of the freezers and defrost it in the microwave. Granny Lynn mixed it with powdered eggs, dehydrated onions, ketchup, and cornflakes, making four giant meatloaves in five-gallon metal steam-table trays.

Just before dinner Cat-Eyes clomped in with his shoddy boots wrapped in duct tape. He was escorting a gray-haired man wearing a light jacket and torn sneakers with no laces, carrying a sheaf of paperwork in a wet paper bag. There was a bloodied bandage on his throat, and his eyes were rheumy.

"The cop said they found him sitting at the bus stop in front of the hospital," Cat-Eyes told me. He said the man's name was Wilbur, and that he didn't talk much. He put a hand under the old man's elbow to steady him. Wilbur swayed a little, then fell back into Cat-Eyes's arms.

Wilbur spent the night on the floor of the office, bundled in a worn mattress pad and my mother's parka. He seemed too frail to leave in the hallway with the other latecomers, who were restless with drink or delusion and hadn't wanted to come inside at all. I sat perched in the desk chair after lights-out, listening to him breathe. It seemed possible that, at some point in the night, his breathing would stop. The papers he'd been carrying were prescriptions and discharge orders, and the bloody bandage covered the hole where he'd had a feeding tube until just that morning. A tumor the size of a loaf of bread hung over the belt of his pants. Stomach cancer, he told me. "I probably won't live till spring," he'd said during the intake process, as if it were just another piece of information for the form. "But the medical card only pays for so many days in the hospital, and I guess my days ran out this morning." He smiled, then turned his hands up in a gesture of helplessness.

Wilbur either never had been, or always was, homeless, depending on how you view private property. He lived in the same tar-paper shack he'd been raised in, but he didn't own it. His family had been squatting on unused coal company land in Preston County, West Virginia, for three generations. He'd worked odd jobs and done some coal mining, but mostly he lived off what he could grow, hunt, and—since his sixty-fifth birthday a few months before—buy with his meager Social Security check. He drank some but wasn't a drunk. He didn't read well but had never needed to learn. He wasn't much of a churchgoing man, because the church was a long walk from his home and he'd never owned a car, but he said his prayers and figured he was mostly right with God. His life seemed to suit him. Or it had, until the cancer forced him into town.

I'd heard a lot of tragic stories in my year at Bartlett House, and I knew that almost everyone at the shelter wouldn't have ended up there if jobs were easier to come by. Or if we hadn't stopped building low-income housing. Or if we still believed the middle and upper classes are obligated to offer a hand to the impoverished. Or if we'd followed through on the promise to build full-service community mental health centers for the people who'd been released from our asylums and state hospitals. But I also knew some details that made their homelessness more than just the inevitable result of a failing social welfare system: the women who used the shelter to get away from one abusive man only to leave with another a few weeks later, the old men who had to drink just to get by, the young men and women who were mentally ill and used street drugs but didn't take the pills prescribed to treat their conditions. The people who came through Bartlett House had difficult lives and complicated stories. My job was just to feed them, assign them chores and a bed, and keep the peace as best I could.

Wilbur was a single man who had lived in the country until cancer made him too weak to hunt or farm. He hadn't ended up at the homeless shelter because he'd drunk himself there, squandered his money, or been caught cheating on a disability claim. No, Wilbur had ended up at Bartlett House because he'd never married or had children, and kin was how a man like Wilbur made it through the final years of his life.

Since my late teens I'd been the sort of hippie who thinks saving the world consists of doing bong hits and going to Rainbow Gatherings. Before moving to Morgantown, I'd lived for a while in rural Wayne County on a commune that had electricity but no running water. We showered by standing under a dribble of lukewarm water from a bucket on a hook, and we woke up in the early morning hours to add logs to the woodstove. We tried to feed ourselves solely on what we could grow on the one small patch of bottomland near the well—and failed. It had been worthwhile, but the world had stayed the same in spite of our sacrifices.

By my late twenties, I was trying to help improve the world by supporting my community. I put "Think Globally/Act

Locally" and "Who Is Your Farmer?" bumper stickers on my car. I stopped shopping at chain grocery stores in favor of the local co-op and bought clothes only in thrift stores. And yet the world didn't seem to change for the better.

So, when a man dying of cancer showed up at the homeless shelter one snowy night in a thin jacket and with no place to go, I decided to offer him the empty basement apartment in my house. The doctors said he had only weeks to live. *How much of a burden could a few weeks be*, I thought.

It was surprisingly easy to convince the officials to let me bend the rules about client-staff interaction and take Wilbur home with me. Even people with long careers in social services—and the disillusionment that comes with them—understood that Wilbur's life shouldn't end at Bartlett House.

The basement apartment was a dump, even compared to the rest of my ramshackle little house. When I'd first bought the place, which had no central heating and cost only 24,000 dollars, I rented the apartment out to a writer, who thought it romantically rustic, for a hundred dollars a month. After he moved out, I'd left it empty with the vague plan, but neither the skill nor the money, to fix it up. The floor was a concrete slab, the walls crumbling drywall or exposed cinderblock. The bathroom had only a toilet and a miner's shower—a showerhead attached directly to a pipe in the ceiling—but Wilbur's old shack had neither running water nor electricity. The apartment also had its own street-level entrance with a wide porch shaded by an apple tree and lined with a row of forsythia bushes, both of which bloomed at the end of winter, almost the instant the snow from the storm had melted. "I like to sit out on the porch of an evening and have me a sip of beer," Wilbur said upon seeing the place. I understood that to mean he was satisfied with it.

Less than two weeks after the police had brought Wilbur to the shelter, I moved him into the apartment. Wilbur was fastidious about his new home. He spent his Social Security check on curtains, a slipcover for the tattered sleeper sofa in the living room, and bottles of bleach and boxes of steel wool. The social worker from Bartlett House found him dishes, sheets, a half-busted vacuum cleaner, and a television. The grants director from the state sent him two ferns as a housewarming gift. Virgil Peterson, an English professor at the local university with whom I'd taken a class, provided a mattress and box spring he said were used and just lying around his house, but they smelled as though they were freshly removed from the plastic wrappings in which they'd been packaged. Rich, the overnight shelter worker, borrowed a truck and drove Wilbur to retrieve what he wanted from the tar-paper shack. Merely a few weeks after he'd been released from the hospital, Wilbur was now back on his feet.

Wilbur was also fastidious about his appearance. He kept his thick white hair in a pomaded pompadour and wore Western shirts and jeans—both of which he kept ironed—and belts with large brass buckles that he shined and white leather tennis shoes that he polished. "If a man doesn't want people to treat him like a bum, he can't look like one," he said. And he didn't look like a bum. He looked like an aging country-music star—the kind who had a storied past but had grown temperate and dignified with age.

The cancer hadn't killed Wilbur by late spring of that year. Or the next. For as long as I lived in that little house with the basement apartment, he did, too. He was rarely any trouble. Once in a while, he'd go downtown and forget that, due to the cancer, his body couldn't tolerate more than two beers. He'd have four or five and then start the walk home only to discover he was too tired to make it. The police would find him asleep on a bench in the courthouse square. When they woke him, he'd say, "Call my daughter, Sarah." The police, who knew I wasn't his child, would call and say jokingly, "We need you to come and get your father." When I'd arrive to pick him up from the station, Wilbur would hug me and wink, as if he thought we'd really pulled one over on the man. The police winked, too, as though we'd just pulled one over on Wilbur. And I would smile, because I knew nobody was getting the raw end of the deal.

In addition to my shifts at Bartlett House, I was taking classes and working toward my college degree at the time, so I wasn't home much. Early on I gave Wilbur a key to my door and an extra set of keys to my junker of a car, because he liked to work on it when I left it at home. On Wednesdays, while I was at the shelter, Wilbur let himself into my kitchen to use the washing machine and hung his clothes to dry on a line he'd strung from the apple tree to the side of the house. When the washing machine broke down, which it did every few months, he fixed it. He was handy, and often came upstairs to fiddle with the plumbing, the old heaters, or the fuse box. Though he'd never owned a car, he kept my oil changed. And although he couldn't push the lawnmower, due to his health, he kept the blades sharp for me and made sure it was full of gas. Because he couldn't write well, he left me artifacts instead of notes: empty oil cans, the busted belt he'd replaced on the washer, or a bouquet of wildflowers wrapped in a paper towel on my kitchen table.

Every Saturday, I brought him groceries: twenty-one cans of chocolate Ensure, two Hershey's chocolate bars, and seven forty-ounce bottles of malt liquor. We'd sit on the porch or stand in the kitchen and gossip about the goings-on at the shelter. The folks who cycled in and out at Bartlett House were the closest he had to friends since moving into town. Two or three times a week, he'd go to the soup kitchen for a lunch he couldn't eat, just for the company. He would warn me when Traveling Jack was on a drinking binge and ought to be put out at night, when Pamela was off her meds and needed looking after, or when there was someone new in town who he thought was up to no good and warranted extra scrutiny. He knew, without being told, that he shouldn't bring these friends back to my house. If they gave him flak about this, he never let on, though I imagine they did. Apartments tend to be communal among the frequently homeless, which is partly why it's so hard for them to hold on to apartments once they get them.

When Wilbur was undergoing chemotherapy, I took him to the hospital twice a week. He told me that, because he got the poison so slowly, it never made him ill, but he refused radiation treatment after the first course. Given the odds, he didn't think the sickness and discomfort it caused was worth it. "If I was a dog, it wouldn't be time to put me down, but there wouldn't be no use in taking me to the vet, neither," he joked. He was proud of outlasting his doctor's prognosis. He refused pain medication because the physician told him he couldn't drink alcohol while taking it and that offended his sense of autonomy. Wilbur told me he usually fell asleep with the beer bottle still mostly full and he dumped out the rest in the morning, but it was the principle of the thing. "Ain't nobody," he'd say, "should tell an old man he can't have himself a beer at night, excepting his wife." And, he added, he'd never wanted a wife.

I was twenty-nine the summer I finished college — long after Wilbur should have been dead, according to his doctor — and I sold the house and moved to Alabama. I felt guilty leaving Wilbur behind, with nobody to drive him to the hospital or do his shopping.

"Do you want to come with me?" I'd asked, once my decision was made. "You can. And it's always warm there, which would be easier on you." We were standing in his kitchen, both in aprons. I was making pies for a bake sale, and he was teaching me how to make the crust with lard, the way his mother had.

"Nah," he said, cutting the lard into the flour with two knives. "I like it here just fine, and I can get along." He told me the ladies from Christian Help would take him to the doctor and that he was sure he could find someone to do his shopping. He passed me the mixing bowl and said he'd never been any good at rolling out the crust.

He didn't seem sick, just worn out. He'd never really seemed sick after that first night in the shelter.

"I feel like I'm running out on you, though. Maybe I shouldn't go?"

"Now you're just talking crazy," he said, taking off his apron. He told me to finish the pies and said he was going to lie down for a nap. He ducked out of the kitchen without even saying goodbye, and, just like that, the matter was settled.

I knocked five thousand dollars off the price of the house and sold it to some friends with the agreement that Wilbur could stay there rent-free for as long as he lived. They promised to be kind to him, though not to take him to doctor's appointments or do his shopping. I called to check on him as soon as I'd moved into my new place. The friends who bought the house carried their cordless phone down to him. "You just get on with your life," he said. "I've got everything under control here. Now quit bothering me and these nice people and get you some rest."

Wilbur died two weeks later, sitting in an old armchair that he'd found in a neighbor's trash and moved onto the porch just that afternoon. He had a pauper's burial, but then, I'd never known him to be much for ceremony. The social worker at Bartlett House filled out the forms, even though it had been years since Wilbur had been her responsibility. There was no funeral service. No headstone. Just a short prayer before lunch at the soup kitchen on the day he was buried.

What I Know of Madness

The Trans-Allegheny Lunatic Asylum

The minute we turn off Meathouse Fork Road, the Appalachian mountain roads go all one-lane and twisty. My night vision isn't good, there are deer around every turn and switch-back, and locals who could drive this stretch of road blind are impatient behind me. But my friend Brad is kind. He just laughs a little when I say that this might be the scariest part of our planned ghost-hunting adventure.

By the time we arrive in Weston, West Virginia, it is good and truly dark and I can't see far enough beyond the gleam of headlights to get my bearings, so Brad takes over as navigator.

"Which way should I turn?" I ask.

"Left," he answers.

"And now?" I ask.

"And now?"

He guides us to a CVS, though how I don't know. Something about the way the streets lay out makes sense to him in a way it doesn't to me. I buy flashlights, because it's only just now dawned on me that the old state hospital in which we're about to spend the night probably doesn't have electricity. We'll be glad for them later, because—except for a break room and two bathrooms—it doesn't.

The guy at the counter is in his mid-fifties, with the lilting accent of central West Virginia, and so I tell him where we're going because I hope he'll have stories.

"You're doing the ghost hunting tour at the old hospital?" he asks, after I've just said we are. He doesn't say asylum, like the website does, or mental hospital, the colloquialism with which I grew up in hills not far from here. The hospital—first, the old one we're going to visit, and then the new one which took its place a little more than a decade ago only a few miles away—has always been the lifeblood of this little Appalachian town, and so the locals afford it as much dignity as they can.

"I remember when I was about fifteen or sixteen," he tells us, "walking down the sidewalk beside the fence at the hospital when I should have been at school. There was this lady there, one of the patients, and she kept pulling up her skirt and her stockings." He pantomimes a woman lifting her skirt up above her hips and showing off the tops of her stockings seductively. "I said, 'Lady, I'm only about fifteen years old. You ought not to be doing that.'" He laughs. "But I remembered it all these years. Yes sir, I never did forget it."

This may be the only true story we'll hear tonight about the patients at the Weston State Hospital, now a "historic" and "paranormal" tourist destination operating under its original name: The Trans-Allegheny Lunatic Asylum.

Arriving

Copperhead, a man with long red-grey hair in faded jeans, boots, and lots of faux-pagan jewelry, calls everybody out into the main hallway when it's time for the tour to begin. "We got a few rules we need to go over first," he says, his thumbs hooked into his belt loops. The rules are simple. Don't take food out of the break room, because they're tired of having to clean up after people. Don't smoke except in the two designated areas; outside through the doors behind us or on the second-floor balcony just off the old doctor's quarters. No drugs or alcohol, even if you brought enough to share. He explains that we'll be split into two groups of twelve. One group will start on the first two floors, the second on floors three and four. After an hour or so with our guide, we'll be free to split up and explore those floors of the hospital on our own. After four hours, at 1 a.m., we'll switch floors. The tour lasts from 9 p.m. to 5 a.m. "And be respectful," he says. "These ghosts were people. Are still people. Don't provoke them." Then he smiles a carnival-barker smile and says, "If you want to know what I mean by provoke 'em, I mean don't act like Zak." Everyone else in the crowd laughs. Brad and I look at each other. Neither of us has any idea who Zak is.

The Guide

Sarah, a short middle-aged woman in sweatpants and an OK Kitty scarf, tells us she drove for more than an hour to be our tour guide, spending pretty much all of the sixty dollars she'll be paid for the night in gas to get here. When I ask her why she'd do that, she says she loves the building. And it is an amazing building, nearly a quarter mile long, with beautiful hand carved woodwork and unexpected beaux-arts touches. Sarah says it's the largest hand-cut stone building in North America. Even this claim, when I try to verify it, proves elusive. It all comes down to how one defines largest.

"I read that the workers who broke ground on the hospital

were 'Negro convict labor' (I make air quotes because I'm incapable of using the word Negro without them), slaves who'd been set free when West Virginia broke with Virginia, but who were then immediately arrested for being vagrants and put to work by the new state," I tell her. "Is that true?"

"Oh, God, I never heard that," she says, shaking her head. "It could be. We don't like to talk about the more unpleasant parts of the hospital's history."

Floors 1 and 2

The first ghosts Sarah introduces to us are Lilly, Ruth, and Emily. Lilly and Emily are both little girls, and both—they say—will come out to play with lucky ghost hunters. Ruth is an old woman, and the only impairment we're told about is that she was confined to a feeding chair, a sort of wheelchair with a tray attached to the front. The guide suggests that sometimes visitors hear the sound of it going up and down the halls. We're told she's protective of the child-ghosts. A domestic haunting. There are music boxes in the rooms both girls are said to haunt; the cheap reproductions every little girl has with the plastic ballerina en pointe twirling in the middle. In Lilly's room, there is also a toy box full of cheap plastic toys, which our guide tells us have been brought and left for the girl-ghost by visitors. Someone in our crowd says, "Like she'd even know what to do with toys from the twentieth century." I want to answer, "There were children here until 1994, as patients," but I'm still trying to behave, to blend in, so I don't. Instead, I ask Sarah, "Were these real patients here? Do you know when and why they were here?"

"We don't talk about patient history," Sarah tells me. "That's not what people come here for. Even on the historical tour, we stick to talking about the building, about the treatments, and about some of the notable staff."

The only other named ghost on the first two floors is Jacob, an alcoholic who responds well to being offered whiskey. Which, of course, we've been told it is against the rules for us to have. And maybe it really is, because although there are many moldering and melted pieces of candy on the windowsills of the girl ghost's rooms, there are no half-full whiskey bottles in Jacob's.

After about an hour of this, Sarah lets us loose on our own, allowing us to wander the entire building—save for a few rooms whose doors are locked because the floors have become unsafe—unescorted. The building is 242,000 square feet; most of the time we are too far away from the other ghost hunters to even hear them.

"This is the part that feels really transgressive," I say to Brad as we wander alone down a dark corridor. "It doesn't seem like we should be allowed to do this." I open the door to a large bathroom with several toilet stalls, baths, and sinks.

"Yeah," Brad says. "But I guess there isn't much we could do to the place." He shines his flashlight into a pile of debris in the far corner of the hallway.

I step into the bathroom. "You know, I was always too

afraid to do this as a kid," I say and then look into the mirror. "Bloody Mary," I say and then spin around. "Bloody Mary." Spin. "Bloody Mary." Spin. No apparition appears in the mirror. I knew it wouldn't, but for a moment there had been a frisson of fear in my belly, an echo of a younger me who was capable of believing in ghosts.

What I Know of Madness 1

I am in an unlit room, sitting on a rocking chair in front of a barred window, looking out over a darkened lawn. I wear a white cotton nightgown with flocking around the banded collar and hold my mother's old porcelain doll—the one she named Baby Brother—in my arms. His skull is bald and crazed with age, the paint that gave detail to his face long ago rubbed away. I have wrapped him in a white blanket, and I am singing tunelessly to him while I rock.

In this dream, one I've had now and again for twenty years, a series of doctors come into the room and insist Baby Brother isn't a real baby, that I must put him down and come away, and I will be locked in this room until I do. I both know and don't know the doll is not a real baby. That it is not my baby. It doesn't matter. The idea of letting him go is a searing pain across my chest. Each time they try to pry him from my arms, I want to scream, the pain so strong it takes my breath away. It is unbearable and I turn my head to look out into the starless night.

I want to say, "I know he isn't real, and it doesn't matter." I want to say, "This isn't something you could understand." But I can't, because every time they walk into the room they reach for the doll, and then I have no breath for words.

What Lingers

For the first hour of the tour, I think that the most abject thing about the old hospital is that it still stinks of stale sweat and filthy bodies. But then we're allowed to go off by ourselves, and the smell dies. When we get back together, I realize it's one of the other tourists…a big guy in unwashed jeans who has been here before and who believes not only that there are ghosts here, but that he has a special ability to find them. He calls himself a ghost hunter with pride, not irony.

The Lobotomy Recovery Ward

The lobotomy recovery ward is not on the walk-through of the first two floors that Sarah led us on, but neither is it off limits, so we ask Copperhead to tell us how to find it. "I'll walk you down," he says. I try to ask him questions, but he's got a salesman's heavy handed way of answering that always turns the question back around to his own prowess as a ghost hunter. "We find the ghosts from talking to them, interacting with them, not by reading the records. But often, we can match the ghosts we find with someone in the actual patient registry. Like Jacob," he says, referring to the one male ghost in the first two levels. "We found that there was in fact a Jacob here being treated for alcoholism, and that he was obsessed with talking about whiskey." This is rural Appalachia. If there had never been a drunk named Jacob in treatment here during the more than 100 years the hospital operated, that would be the coincidence worth noting.

Lobotomies at Weston Hospital were most often performed by Dr. Walter Freeman, the doctor who "pioneered" the ice pick lobotomy. He traveled around the country in his personal van, which he called the lobotomobile, performing procedures at a number of institutions.

"When did they stop doing lobotomies here?" I ask Copperhead. A few yards ahead, he points to a plaque about Dr. Freeman, which says he performed his last lobotomy at Weston in 1967. "There, see, it says. 1967." But I know this sign elides a more difficult truth. Dr. Freeman's last lobotomy procedure at Weston was in 1967, but I know a woman who was the head nurse in the lobotomy recovery ward in the 1980s. I tell Copperhead this.

"That can't be true," he says, turning his back to me and walking on. "The sign says right there, the last one was done in 1967."

Freeman was no longer performing the surgeries, but other physicians were. I don't think Copperhead is lying, I just don't think he knows very much about the actual history of the hospital. Or cares, and that troubles me more.

Brad and I have borrowed something called a "k2," a meter that's supposed to read electro-magnetic energy and thus identify the presence of ghosts. It looks like a television remote with no buttons; just a row of five lights: green, light green, yellow, orange, and red. Just what these lights mean is vague, except that the more of them that are lit up, the more it suggests the presence of a spirit. The whole time we're in the lobotomy ward, all five of the lights on ours stay lit.

"What kind of activity do you get down here? Do the ghosts speak to you?" Brad asks Copperhead.

"No. I mean, these guys were pretty much brain-dead, so we don't get much from them," Copperhead says.

What I Know of Madness 2

In my dream, the bars on the window blur, and I stare beyond the darkened lawn to a row of Bald Cypress trees. These twisted giants shielded my childhood. I remember playing in their towering ranks, hiding with Felicity when we were still small enough to stand among their knees and not be seen.

I am not at Cypress Manor, although these are my grandfather's trees and not simply the same kind. I don't know how they have come to line the lawn of this sterile place, with its white blankets, white paint, and doctors in quiet white shoes. I'm not sure if the trees are meant to keep me safely here or mark the border to the place I could go if I would just put down the doll. It doesn't matter.

I hold Baby Brother in my lap and stare out over the darkened lawn at the silhouettes of these magnificent trees until the doctors give up and leave the room. In the quiet, I weep at the sweetness of being among the cypress again, and now it's the pain of their beauty that takes my breath away. I can't imagine wanting to leave this place, to ever again live beyond the reach of their long shadows. I laugh at the doctors for threatening to keep me locked in. If they want the doll, they should threaten to throw the door open wide.

I rock the doll, my lips against the warm, downy skin of his scalp. He smells of sweet milk and talc. I hum the song of the wind in the boughs of the trees, rocking back and forth in rhythm with their gentle sway.

The One Story They Claim is True

"Dean," Sarah says, "was a mute. This story, we can document. This one, we know is true. His roommates hung him from the ceiling with a bed sheet and beat him, beat him real bad. One of them realized that they were going to get in big trouble, so they decided they better kill him. Dean was unconscious, so they laid him on the floor and put the leg of one of the beds on his head. Then they jumped up and down on the bed until they had pulverized his skull." She pauses for effect. "Then one of his two roommates ran down the hall to the nurse's station and said that the ghost in this room had killed Dean. One of the men who did it, a man named Myers, just died at the new Sharpe state hospital a couple of weeks ago.

"When we first started coming through here, Dean was real friendly. He'd play with us and joke around. But over time, he got quieter and quieter until finally he just stopped interacting with us at all. We asked him if we'd hurt his feelings or offended him. It took Copperhead a while to get him to talk to us, but finally he said no, we hadn't hurt his feelings or anything. It was just hard for him to listen to us tell his story over and over again. So we asked if he wanted us to stop telling people his story. 'No,' he said. 'I think it's important for people to know my story. But could you tell it in the hallway so I don't have to listen to it?' And that," says our guide, "is why we're standing out here instead of in the room."

Brad asks, "Does he communicate any differently with you than the other ghosts, since he couldn't speak?"

"No, I don't think so. What do you mean?" Sarah asks.

"Well, because he wasn't able to talk in life. Like, how did he let you know that he didn't want to listen to you tell his story anymore?"

Sarah is visibly flustered. "Well, Dean has never spoken directly to me. But I'm pretty sure Copperhead and some of the other ghost hunters were able to get his voice on EVP." She explains that it's a sort of tape recorder that can capture ghostly voices and make them audible to us.

I ask Sarah for the full name of Dean's killer, the one who has just died, but she doesn't know. Later, I ask Copperhead. "Michael David Myers," he says. This is the name of the non-speaking serial killer who escapes from a psychiatric hospital to find and kill his sister (and a lot of other people) in the movie *Halloween* and its nine sequels.

Ghost Adventures

Zak, it turns out, is Zak Bagans, one of the hosts of the show *Ghost Adventures*. I find parts of a seven-hour live broadcast they did on

Halloween, 2009 on YouTube. A former employee of Weston Hospital talks about Ruth, remembers her as a violent old woman who would bang on the tray of her feeding chair whenever a man walked past.

Sarah had shown us the seclusion cells, told us that anyone could have a patient put in one, that patients sometimes stayed locked inside for months at a time. That some of them died. Near midnight, Zak locks three volunteers in the seclusion cells and then starts yelling at a ghost he believes has said "screw you" to the ghost hunters. Nothing much happens. One girl says she felt something brush her hair, tug on her jacket. Zak calls out to the ghost he imagines is there, offering to keep the girl locked up in the seclusion cell for the rest of the night if he will only show himself.

I do a web search. Although fans have requested it, none of the many ghost hunting shows have ever gone to a concentration camp.

What I know of Madness 3

"I was in high school," my father said, "and working in the afternoons, driving the truck to make deliveries for Dad."

My grandfather was a grocery wholesaler. Not the grandfather whose cypress trees guarded my childhood, but my father's father, who was the worst sort of bastard; mean and bigoted and dumb. Who never guarded anyone's childhood.

"And I remember coming home from school. Mom was passed out drunk, and when Dad got home, he said, 'I'm not doing it this time. Johnny, you're going to have to take your mother up to the State Hospital. Just pull up and tell 'em you've got Bonnie Einstein, they'll know what to do with her. Lord knows they've seen her enough times before.' And then Dad and I put her in the back of the truck, with all the empty pallets from the day's delivery, and Dad went off to play golf."

I think my father was drunk himself when he told me this story, in the first years of a decade-long bender that would end only when we, his adult children, committed him to a rehab facility. "I also had to go pick her up. Had to take her something to wear, because they just dumped the patients in these big wards, men and women together, and after not too long the clothes they were wearing when they were admitted would rot off their bodies. They didn't give them hospital gowns or anything. Just left them in those big rooms, naked."

Years later, when he tells me that I've made up this story, I don't question him. I hated my grandmother—a mean old drunk with a sharp tongue and filthy mouth—and by then she'd been dead long enough that he'd taken to calling her *my sainted mother*. And he's haunted enough without my insisting on seeing ghosts he doesn't believe are there.

When I Lived in Manhattan

When I lived in Manhattan, we sat in East Side bars full of books and leather, smoking cigars and drinking Cosmopolitans. We wore our pearls without irony, our hair down long and straight, and our heels high.

When I lived in Manhattan, my mother used to say, "Don't come back to West Virginia and tell us how much better everything is in Manhattan because we don't want to hear about it."

When I lived in Manhattan, Salman Rushdie was our Jay McInerney and we quoted his *Fury* the way teenagers quote songs when they are in love. The city boiled with money and the talk was still of start-ups, IPOs, interactivity, the unimaginable future that had just begun to begin. We carried worn copies of the paperback in our messenger bags and dog-eared the pages that told us we were changing the world.

When I lived in Manhattan, Joey Ramone wrote a song to Maria Bartiromo and, somehow, punk didn't die. Although, shortly thereafter, Joey did.

When I lived in Manhattan, people began living with—rather than dying from–AIDS.

When I lived in Manhattan, I would scour the Green Market for fiddlehead ferns, morels, and ramps in early Spring, cook them up in omelets for my lovers, and talk about how they tasted of home. I'd never actually eaten any of those things until I moved to Manhattan. In West Virginia, we ate our vegetables out of the can.

When I lived in Manhattan, the macaroni and cheese at Chat n Chew was all the rage.

When I lived in Manhattan, Patti Smith was everybody's godmother.

When I lived in Manhattan, the hippest lesbians hung out at Meow Mix in the East Village. It was grungy and boho and all the girls were both younger and cooler than I could have pretended to be, so instead I tried The Cowgirl Hall of Fame where all the lesbians were already married to each other and just stopping by for hamburgers on their way to Lamaze class, so I moved on to the Clit Club at Mother where the drag kings all looked like Elvis and the only person who ever hit on me was a very drunk drag queen who seemed to think I came as a package deal with the attractive young man sitting beside me at the bar. I didn't know that attractive young man, so I didn't really have anything to offer my suitor but at closing time we took ourselves to the Kiev for a consolation breakfast anyway. We became running buddies—hanging out at clubs like Save the Robots and The Limelight—until the night she met the man of her dreams in the bathroom at Candybar, changed into chinos, and moved with him to Brooklyn.

When I lived in Manhattan, most of my lovers were men.

When I lived in Manhattan, the skyline was still intact.

When I lived in Manhattan, certain folk back home said it was about time I moved to Jew York.

When I lived in Manhattan, I used to run across a B-list actress–an older woman who played mostly slightly dopey grandmothers–at the grocery store. In her cart, she would have laundry soap and ground beef and bags of apples and toilet paper and cans of tuna and boxes of pasta and the same brand of shampoo that was supposed to tame frizzy hair that I had in mine. We'd smile and nod if we passed in the aisles. On the rare occasion we'd pass on the street, we just kept walking.

When I lived in Manhattan, everyone liked to tell this joke: In a flat, Midwestern drawl, "They ought to build an island and put all you queers on it." In voice full of joie de vivre, "They did, sweetie, and you're standing on it!"

When I lived in Manhattan, I sent my laundry to the Fluff and Fold.

When I lived in Manhattan, nobody ever said to me, "You wear too much black."

When I lived in Manhattan, we sometimes had champagne and caviar on toast points for lunch.

When I lived in Manhattan, I learned not to say my hair needs washing or the sink needs fixing, to say hollow instead of holler, and that nothing is ever up over yonder.

When I lived in Manhattan, I used to run into Soupy Sales at the bodega on the corner of 33rd and 2nd on a fairly regular basis. We would buy hotdogs and go sit on a bench and reminisce about West Virginia. He'd say, every time, "Man, these New York dogs aren't nearly as good as Stewart's hotdogs," meaning the little local joint back home and not the national chain. And they weren't. Then he'd shake his head and say "Look at us. Two Jews from Huntington sitting in New York. That's not something you see every day." We'd laugh, and then he'd pat me on the shoulder and walk home.

When I lived in Manhattan, we all knew the secret to the soup dumplings at Joe's Shanghai but were willing to pretend that we didn't and to accept them as a miracle of the city.

When I lived in Manhattan, I was for The Mets.

When I lived in Manhattan, and couldn't take the swank bars any more but had outgrown the club kid clubs, I would catch a cab to the Meatpacking District and hang out at Hellfire, a dingy S&M club filled with chubby, middle-aged couples whipping one another and scarred ex-junkies looking to hook up with the PVC clad young women who were on their way to becoming junkies and were just there to earn a little cash. I was part of a small gaggle of hipsters that sat at a corner table, swilling expensive vodka out of a paper sack and smiling at the elderly professor who walked around the club naked and masturbating, though not in an encouraging way, not in a way that would make him think it all right to come over and say hello.

When I lived in Manhattan, Rudy Giuliani was Mayor but Ed Koch was still Queen.

When I lived in Manhattan, a wolf prowled the woods in Central Park.

When I lived in Manhattan, the photographer Gordon Parks was my neighbor and some mornings I would ride down in the elevator with him and his date of the previous evening. He was in his eighties then; the dates—who always seemed to me to be different young women—mostly looked to be in their twenties. One day, having forgotten some paper or file, I rode back up with him after he'd said his goodbyes. "I'm just the right amount of famous," he said, smiling. "I get to go home with the prettiest girl at every party, if I want to, and of course I get invited to every party." He ran his fingers over his thick, white mustache. "But on the street, almost nobody recognizes me, so I don't have to deal with that." I smiled and nodded as the elevator stopped at my floor. I unlocked my door and grabbed the file or paper off my desk, over which I'd hung a copy of Gordon Parks' *American Gothic* long before I knew he was my neighbor.

When I lived in Manhattan, a friend's mother told me that I had almost no accent in English, but that listening to me say the blessing over the candles in Hebrew was like watching a *Beverly Hillbillies Hanukkah Special*.

When I lived in Manhattan, everyone was mad for curried goat.

When I lived in Manhattan, Alan Greenspan was our holy man. When I lived in Manhattan, the last ad agency at which I worked held a lavish Christmas party with a special musical guest. We all worried, over the free lobster on the buffet and with glasses of Moët in our hands, that it might be the president of the company who had his own, not very good, garage band. But it wasn't his band. It was an old man with a square guitar. I squealed, everyone else just look puzzled. I was a little surprised to be the only one at my table to recognize him when he came out on stage, and even more so when I was the only one who recognized him when he began to sing. "That's Bo Diddley," I yelled at them, incredulous. "The legendary Bo Diddley." "Oh," they said, and wandered back to the open bar.

Mot

THE KOA CAMPGROUND IN AMARILLO sits in a surprisingly seedy neighborhood, more urban than I had expected. A very middle-class couple with impossibly wide smiles advertises an adult video and novelty store from a billboard just before the final turn-off to the campground. Cattle graze in a pasture along the road. An unsettling mixture of the bucolic and the pornographic. Rusted trucks sit in the driveways of rusted mobile homes.

    I am here to visit Mot, a new and unlikely friend who wanders from place to place, dragging a coterie of dead relatives, celebrities, Polish folktale villains, and Old Testament gods along with him in his head. He left our home in Morgantown, West Virginia, a month ago, heading for Amarillo, because cars, he said, can be had more cheaply out West, and he needed a car. But more than that, although he didn't say it, he needed to move on. By his own report, he hasn't stayed in any one place for longer than three months in more than thirty years. Friends have sometimes lasted a place or two, never many, but while they are around his voices are quieter, more easily managed. Having someone real to talk with keeps him grounded, he says, and humor helps.

    Our friendship is an experiment for both of us; we are trying to see if it can fend off our individual demons. His the literal sort, mine the metaphorical. Mot is dubious. "There are a lot of bad characters over here," he tells me on the phone, "and most of them don't want you around."

    I originally planned to pitch my tent where he was

camping. Because he had called it camping, I envisioned some uninhabited wilderness just beyond the sprawl of Amarillo. I was wrong. Mot slept behind an abandoned industrial building on a busy thoroughfare. He had few belongings: extra clothes in a small backpack, an old digital camera I'd given him, a few tools, a wooden-handled knife from Dollar Tree. Each morning, he wrapped these things in a tattered black and red woolen blanket he'd found in Romania. Hiding the bundle carefully under a pile of rusted scrap metal near the building, he biked into town to spend the day at the library, at Walmart, or scouting around for a car to buy. In the evening, he retrieved the bundle, stashing the bike in its place. He slept on top of the old blanket, a pillow made of his extra clothes.

  He'd told me all this during a rare call from the pay phone at the public library, and I immediately scoured the web to find someplace more acceptable to stay during my visit. The small one-room cabins and large communal bathrooms of the KOA seemed a workable compromise. I am comfortable with the idea of being bunkmates but not roommates. Neither Mot, nor my husband would mistake bunk beds and communal bathrooms as romantic.

  A few days before I left for Amarillo, Mot bought a complete wreck of a car for $400 from a kid working at an ice-cream store. He broke camp behind the abandoned building and began staying overnight in the parking lots of the four Amarillo Wal-Marts. He sent me an email with a picture of his ancient sedan, gray except for one bright blue door and a bent frame that suggested a tragic past.

I PULL INTO THE KOA AT NOON, having promised to arrive by four. I'm a little surprised Mot isn't here. He and I share a social awkwardness; we are both always early to everything. But I am four hours early, so I'm not worried. I gather fresh clothes and head to the showers to wash away the road. I'm charmed, listening to a young mother as she tries to wrangle her toddling son through the rigors of washing his hair. I have stumbled into an oasis of civility. I had expected the campground to be full of half-drunk bikers and bedraggled women yelling at their children. I'm relieved to have been wrong but also concerned; Mot will most certainly stand out among these vacationing families and senior citizen sunbirds. I do not want anyone to hurt his feelings, and I begin to fear these vacationing Middle Americans might. Folks stop and talk to one another, sharing vacation plans, asking about nearby attractions. I hadn't counted on that. I'm not sure how they will take his just-to-the-left-of-things answers.

The cabin is a medium-sized room with a double bed on one wall, bunk beds on the other, and three shelves. It will be closer for the two of us than I'd imagined. I am won over by the porch, which is wide and sturdy and has a swing. It looks out over a parking lot, some tent sites, and then a stockyard; it is not a lovely view. But the wind in Amarillo amazes me. It gusts with such strength that I spend a few minutes sitting on the swing, catching the breeze in my shawl and letting it pull me back, then releasing it and swinging forward again.

The afternoon sludges by, viscous and sticky inside the cabin. I'm not good at waiting—it invites worry, which I do too well. When there is no sign of Mot at four-thirty, I begin to wonder if he's all right. Finally, at a quarter till six, I cannot sit in the cabin any longer. I ask the guy behind the counter for directions to the nearest Wal-Mart, and he draws a very crude map on a napkin. I know it's a long shot. Mot has told me there are four Wal-Marts in Amarillo, and I am not certain I can find even this one with the directions I've been given. I have no idea what time he usually settles in, or if he's even still in town. I tell myself I'm not going to find him; I am going to pick up a paper and maybe grab some dinner. It sounds less ridiculous.

 Only, in the end, it's not ridiculous at all. I see the old gray sedan with the tragic bent look as soon as I swing into the parking lot. I pull up several feet away and get out of my car cautiously. The very top of a man's head is visible in the driver's side window, but I can't be sure it's Mot. I'm afraid he may have abandoned the car, or given it away, and am worried about what sort of person I might startle if he has. The man in the car is slumped over something I can't see. I slam my car door loudly, but the person doesn't move. I call Mot's name, a question in it, and get no response. Left with no other choice, I walk over to the car and lean in the open window on the

passenger's side.

 There is Mot, pissing into an old soda bottle. He doesn't acknowledge me, and I pull my head out of the car and wait for him to finish. He looks terrible, his hair wild and his face streaked with axle grease and mud. His clothes are filthy and his shirt misbuttoned. He rarely looks his sixty-six years; today he looks that and then some. A pint of Scotch sits open on the seat beside him. When he finishes, he puts the lid on the soda bottle but does not zip his pants. He stares carefully out the windshield, unmoving, and I can't tell if he isn't aware of me or if he is ignoring me.

I have no idea what to do. I have the sick feeling that whatever I do will be the wrong thing, and if it is wrong enough I may send him screaming from the few comforts he's accumulated since he arrived here: the car, the tools to work on it, an extra few sets of clothes. But I must do something.

This is part of why I am here. I am in search of the imperative. Ambiguity erased by urgency. It's a crystalline moment, one in which I know that the only truly unforgivable response would be to fail to act. Instinct, rather than reason or experience, must guide me.

I walk around to the driver's side of the car and open the door. Mot turns his head toward me, looking more over my shoulder than at me, but he doesn't speak. "Hey you," I prod quietly, "aren't you even going to say hello?" He sits for a moment more and finally says "No, I mean, Sarah never showed up so I figure that's that."

"What do you mean, I never showed up? I'm right here. I have been waiting for you at the campground since noon." I don't know what to say once I realize he doesn't think I'm real. "I said I would be here on Monday by 4 o'clock and I was. You just never came to the camp."

At the word Monday, Mot snaps his head around and finally looks at me, anger animating his face. "Yes, but you see, this is Tuesday. I went to the campground on Monday and Sarah was not there." He spits the words at me and cackles. He thinks he has outsmarted whichever of his tormentors has conjured this hallucination of me into being.

"It's not Tuesday," I say firmly. "It's Monday, and I am here exactly like I said I would be." Out of the corner of my eye, I notice a police car swing into an empty space a few yards away, watching.

Mot reaches under the passenger seat and pulls out a greasy newspaper. "No, it is not. Today is Tuesday. See, I have today's paper right here." He smacks the front page soundly with his paralyzed hand and then waves it in front of me, triumphant. I peer in, finding the date on the masthead.

"No, look, right here. It says today is Monday." I point. He looks. He looks again. Suddenly, his features seem to right themselves. He runs his hand through his hair, taming it, and then drops the paper onto his lap, hiding what he suddenly realizes is exposed. "Oh," he says, as if seeing me for the first time, "it's you!"

I move away from the car to give him time to get himself together. I turn my back a few minutes, standing between the sedan and the gaze of the policeman, and then Mot is beside me, his arms outstretched. We hug. He pokes me a few times and sniffs the air near my ear as if to make absolutely certain I am real. "Well, then, let's go to the KOA," he says merrily.

The policeman talks into his radio, his eyes meeting mine as Mot and I finish our hellos, our hugs, and our sheepish apologies. Thinking it would be best to get out of here before the cop notices the open Scotch bottle on Mot's front seat, I agree.

We pull up in front of Kabin 1. "I gotta shower," Mot says the minute we are parked, and gathers the things he needs from the trunk of his car. For half an hour I wait on the swing, rocking back and forth, trying not to decide I have to go home. In the parking lot, I saw more of Mot's illness than I had known was there, and it scares me. I think about his warning. *There are a lot of bad characters over here, and most of them don't want you around.* The reasonable thing would be to offer him the use of the cabin for the time it is already rented, and then simply drive away. But although I can't articulate why I'm here, I am sure it is not to insist that everything be reasonable.

He finally reappears, smiling broadly as if things have gone perfectly so far, and my fear vanishes. He looks younger again, his graying hair neat and just growing out of the military cut he had when he left Morgantown a month ago. His skin is wrinkled and tanned. Freshly washed, and in clean clothes, he looks more like a man with a passion for sailing than one who has been living out of doors for over thirty years. And although a close look will show his left hand is curled into itself, that he drags his left leg a tiny bit, he doesn't look frail, or old, or crazy. He is, in fact, a little handsome.

We talk about not being hungry and decide against wandering off in search of dinner. Instead, we swing. I tell him about the drive, and he reminisces about his own trips down old Route 66. He retrieves the remaining Scotch from the front seat of his car, and I buy a six-pack of beer from the camp store.

We sit outside for a long time, catching up. Night never

seems to fall in Amarillo; dusk stretches on well into what I would have expected to be darkness. A little into the beer, we start reciting poetry for one another. I pull up things memorized during childhood elocution lessons, mostly Emily Dickinson and a little Shakespeare, though not the best of either. Mot's repertoire is more varied. There is Wordsworth, Coleridge, and the inevitable Kipling. We struggle together through "Prufrock," only meeting up as the mermaids are singing each to each. Then Mot begins to recite from a slew of poets I don't know; men who wrote verse about sailing, cattle drives, saloons, and frontiers. He finishes with Robert Service's "The Shooting of Dan McGrew"—a poem I would scoff at except it leaves him damp-eyed and melancholy. Mot's voice, always strong and clear, takes on a brogue that isn't his while he recites, and there is something anachronistic in the whole thing; he isn't old enough to have lived through the world of these poems, but he seems to remember it.

Once we have downed the Scotch and most of the beer, I screw up my courage and ask him what happened to make him lose a day. Asking about the goings-on in Mot's peculiar universe is always risky—speaking of the Big Guys Upstairs can sometimes summon them.

"I don't know. They can just do that. Drop me down into a dark hole so that I can't see or hear anything, and then when I wake up I'm confused and don't know what day it is or anything." His tone says this should be obvious, and I've asked a silly question.

I'm always a little startled by how matter-of-fact he is about his delusions; how he forgets I don't have a direct line into what's going on. "Who dropped you into a hole?"

"It was probably Moloch, but I don't know. Coulda been the girls. The Harpies were all excited that you were on your way. They figure they can use you to finally turn me into a girl, because I like you, and we want to be like the people we find likable, right?" He laughs. "I mean, I don't want to be a girl, but there you have it. They think it's a done deal up here." He motions upwards with his thumb.

The daedal hand of delusion paints everything that happens to Mot on an epic scale. Over the months of our friendship, I have learned enough about the characters to follow his stories; like reading *The Brothers Karamazov,* most of the trick is keeping the names straight.

"I tried to talk Kaiser Bill or Moloch into helping me out, because they don't want to be girls either, and if I'm a girl, then they'll have to be girls, too. But they said nope. Said if I'm going to be a stupid Polack, a Jew lover, I'll just have to be a girl, then. I told you, they don't like Jews, so they don't think I should have anything to do with you." He shrugs and smiles at me. "I guess there is no hope. It's a done deal."

I don't know what to say, so I open the last two beers. Music from a nearby cabin floats by as the wind changes direction, and suddenly Mot is singing to me. Old songs. Cowboy songs, country songs, even church songs. He sings until the beer bottles are empty. I'm afraid someone might come out and complain about the noise, but his voice is good and no one does.

ONCE MOT AND I ARE COMFORTABLE with each other again, we fall back into our Morgantown pattern of non-stop chatter and long drives to no place in particular. Easy conversation and a love of empty hours are part of what binds us together. He is the first friend I've had in years with the time to talk to no purpose or take a drive without a destination. We are, in our time together, aimless and free.

 Mot and I had only the slimmest chance of becoming friends. We met as I was finishing up my months as the director of a drop-in center for adults with mental illness, although most of the forty or so people I saw during a day were homeless junkies coming in to sleep on the couches or use the phone to make a drug connection. Mot avoided such places, but he was already breaking with habit in staying at the local homeless shelter.

 If we hadn't been the only place in town that gave out free coffee without talking about Jesus, I doubt I would have met Mot. One day he sat down in the chair next to my desk and complimented me on my shoes, shoes I was inordinately proud of because they were, in fact, very good shoes. He talked about his own shoes, which he didn't like, and a pair of boots he had loved but worn out walking across Albania. It was the best story I'd heard since I came to Friendship Room. I spent the afternoon listening to him talk about his travels: camping in a bombed-out Italian monastery; the pretty girls in Nice who gave him wine and books written in English; the students in Turkey who had been sure he was someone famous and insisted he come stay with them for a few days. After that, I couldn't stop listening to him.

Two more weeks would go by before I would decide to quit, and then only after a very frightening, very ill man cornered me in the hallway, choked me, and fondled my breasts. When he moved the arm pinning me to the wall by my throat to grab his penis, I pushed him out the door and locked it. Defeated, I wrote my resignation letter while I waited for the police.

Mot's company got me through the first of the months between my resignation and my actual leave-taking. Often, only the prospect of conversations with Mot—conversations about books, travel, art, and eventually the very literary world of his delusions—got me out the door of my house, and into my car, on my way to work. At any time, his stories would have been a joy. At that time, they were all that kept me from being someone who one day walked away from her desk and, without a word, never went back.

I am on this trip, in part, to get away from there for a while and burn up the vacation time I have accumulated over the last year. But this is just an excuse. I don't know why the first real friend I have made in many years is a mentally ill, homeless man who is twenty-five years my senior. This is a question that needs an answer, and I've come to try and find it.

ON MY FIRST MORNING IN AMARILLO, Mot takes me to a diner he says has wonderful waffles. This is a surprise, because it bothers Mot that I am fat much more than it bothers me. Amarillo turns out to be the perfect place for our visit. There is nothing much to do except drive out to Lake Meredith, look around, make plans to camp out one night without ever meaning to actually do it, take pictures, and talk. Most of the time, I give the keys to Mot. Behind the wheel, he is more centered; he takes on a family-man-out-for-a-drive persona, pulls up a part of himself he has imagined, but not lived, and tries to make it real. Beside him, I am also someone else; a person with hours to kill and not much that needs to be done. Relaxed. Companionable. Happy.

We don't get out of the car often, only now and then to look more closely at the desert flowers or to walk around the mostly-empty marina. He knows the names of everything. He does not like the ever-present yucca, finds its seedpod obscene, but delights in showing me my first roadrunner and explaining the dangers of camping in the arroyos. He points out cottonwood, soapberry, and sandbar willows, explains how the white limestone caprock keeps its place as the softer rock beneath erodes. He holds small spiders in his palm and talks about the different kinds of silk they use in spinning their webs. Occasionally, to turn me in the right direction to see a thing, he takes my hand or puts his arm on my shoulder. These small affections, at first awkward, soon grow natural.

Mot's knowledge is encyclopedic; perfect recall seems to be a part of his illness, a kind of compensation for the tricks his mind plays when he tries to string all the events of his life together into a narrative that makes sense. When he isn't teaching me the landscape, he tells me stories from what is left of his past. Most often, he tells the ones about how he came to be a vessel for the

Others. Those stories are hard to hear but are key to understanding the eidola that plague him now. The details in them never change, he recites them the same way he recited "The Shooting of Dan McGrew." He can, if I ask him while he's in the midst of one, tell me the color of the shirt he was wearing or what smells were in the air. The skeleton of his life is there, intact, but the connective tissue is all delusion, stories his mind tells itself to explain the horrible truths in his past. It's the why of things that gives him so much trouble.

I remember when I was five; my mother took me to the movies. She took just me, not any of my brothers or sisters, and she let me pick out the kind of candy I wanted, and then what was really great was she let me hold her hand all through the movie. I was so happy; I thought she finally loved me. But then, after the movie, we went home and she told me to get into the oven. I mean, I told you, I wasn't supposed to be born. Moloch and Dubja had told her that I was supposed to be a girl. I can remember while I was in the womb, she taught me all kinds of things, like how to knit, and showed me the pretty dresses she was making for me. But I wasn't a girl, so she had to get rid of me. I mean, if I wasn't a girl, then I wasn't the promised one, so I was a mistake. She told me it wouldn't hurt, and not to be scared, so I wasn't. I remember the way the grill felt against my cheek. She must have turned on the gas, because I don't remember anything else until our house was full of people. Even my dad had come rushing home from work, and Dr. Dash was there taking care of me. It was the first time they took her away to the hospital. She didn't come back for a long time.

He tells me it's okay to cry, that he understands why someone would cry at a story like this. But I don't, at least not then. I can see The Big Guys Upstairs lurking behind Mot's words, and I don't want to give them anything they can use against him. Just as they are watching me, I've had to learn to watch them and to know their tricks. They use the tears of the women he has known to punish him—he often hears them sobbing quietly behind the other voices—and I won't add my tears to theirs. I save them until I am safely home.

I believe Mot's stories; the one about being put in an oven and another one he's told me about his aunt tying his shoe laces together and telling him to run down the stairs. In that story he falls down the steps and comes back upstairs with a Jesus inside and the ability to tell time. I don't doubt that the spirits of his dead aunts live in the moles on his body, and that the Harpies can send him back down the stairs and into a blackout whenever they want. It's the cosmological argument for The Big Guys Upstairs: because there is a Mot, there must also be a Moloch, a Jack, Dubja, the Harpies, and the Dead Aunts—the ones who created him and control him and without whom he would be plain old Tom again, the Tom he started out to be. I accept this on faith and hope that acceptance will grow into understanding. And because I believe, he can talk to me, and we can be friends. Maybe this, too, is one of the lessons I am here to learn. To listen, not to doubt or give advice, but to simply hear and accept.

THESE ARE THE THINGS WE DO MOST DAYS: go to Wal-Mart, to the lake, swim in the pool at the campground, and cook a supper of lentils and rice on a camp stove at the cabin. We aren't eating lentils and rice for health, or to save money, but because we can't find any good alternatives. We have looked for, but not found, a decent restaurant near the campground. Amarillo seems to be a city on its way out. Every evening, we consider the Asian restaurants and taco stands near the campground, but they look too seedy to me, too much a part of the falling-apartness of the neighborhood we are in, and I am afraid to go inside. Mot doesn't understand this, but he allows it. "I'm not wanted anywhere," he says, "so it doesn't matter. I just go wherever I want."

We do eat at an obvious tourist trap toward the middle of the week, The Big Texan Steak Ranch. It's one of those places with its own gift shop and billboards fifty miles out in every direction. It has a 72-ounce steak that, if devoured completely within an hour, is free. Hostesses dressed like cowgirls and a roving string band dart between the tables of out-of-towners. We order reasonably sized steaks and a bottle of good wine. It's like being in the car, a part of Mot that never gets to show itself comes out and all signs of the Others disappear. We have a good time.

The visit is like this, mostly made up of these small moments of grace when it seems like things might be better than they have been for both of us. That perhaps Mot will be able to have and keep a friend, that maybe my faith in the dignity of those living marginal lives will be restored.

THE RICH STEAKHOUSE DINNER doesn't sit well, and I'm up and down all night. Careful not to wake Mot, I search in the dark for my left shoe, my jacket. Under the red and black blanket, he sleeps on his belly like a baby in a crib—one hand by his face, the other tossed far out to the side. His breathing is soft and shallow; he doesn't snore. He looks deceptively peaceful. Nothing suggests that he's battling demons or reliving old terrors. But he is. He's told me The Others launch their real assault against him at night and not to be frightened if he calls out in his sleep or seems to struggle. He's been told he screams and thrashes around in his sleep. But here in Amarillo, he doesn't fight at all. Instead, he's unnaturally still.

Between bouts of intestinal distress, I curl up sleeplessly in my bed and try to imagine Mot's dreams. Watching him fills me with an aching tenderness, a little maternal and dangerously close to love.

Mot believes we all share the same dreamscape and that when I appear, I am me, acting with volition, and will remember everything that happened when I awake. He holds me accountable. This terrifies and fascinates me. So far, he has only told me of two dreams that include me and in both I was helpful to him. Together, he says, we were able to hold The Others at bay. I suspect this is part of the trick—if I'm an ally now, later when the illness creates dreams in which I betray him it will be more hurtful—and so I don't take credit for whatever help he thinks I've given. "That's not me, no matter what they say, you know," I argue, but he won't listen. He tells me to reread Jung if I won't take his word for it.

When the sun finally rises, I head to the pool. After a night of lying quietly awake, I crave movement and noise. Cold water snaps the tiredness out of my bones; my head clears with the splash of each stroke. At home, I won't swim, too vain to expose my pale, middle-aged body. Here, anonymity defeats my vanity. I spend the morning gliding through the water until I am empty-headed and my muscles are loose and warm, sunning myself on a towel between sets of laps. When I can't swim anymore and my skin is pink and tender, I gather my things and head back to the cabin.

Mot has made us a breakfast of coffee and papaya. He hands me a cup as I walk onto the porch.

"How did you sleep?" I ask, throwing on an old denim shirt I'd stolen from my husband and a pair of shorts over my swimsuit. We sit down on the swing, balancing the plate of papaya chunks between us.

"Lousy. Of course." He rolls his eyes. "A lot going on up here. Mostly the Harpies, but also Dubja and old Willie. Something's up, but they won't clue me in on what's happening. That's how things go. I'm not supposed to know anything."

Since I've been here, the Harpies have dominated his dreams. A collective made up of all the women he has known, they speak as one and don't seem to have any real power. The men in his mind give orders, make things happen. The women can only weep and beg.

"They can only manifest as animals on our plane of existence," Mot explained when he first told me about the Harpies. "That's why animals can talk to me, which is pretty scary. I mean, what does an animal have to say that I want to hear?" He also tells me they run a publishing house in the Northeast. I don't ask how the two things can both be true; he'd have to find a way to explain it, and the explanation would become another layer of the delusion. But I'm amused, imagining a publishing house run by housecats and shrews.

He sips his coffee and stares out at the cows in the nearby stockyard. "They say you're a soul sister and they are trying to warn you about the bad characters over here," he says, gesturing upwards with his thumb. "You know, that's where you'll end up if I outlive you. You'll be one of them. Only don't be like Harpies. They're not nice women. Most of them just want to get laid, that's why they are always trying to turn me into a girl." He sighs. "That's what I like about you. You're not a woman who gets a few drinks in her and says, 'Let's take off all our clothes!' Kooks like that scare me." He laughs and pats me on the knee.

"What I like about you is that you're always telling me what you like about me," I say, offering him the last piece of papaya, "and you make me breakfast." I also like that sex is out of the question. Mot told me when we first met that he's been celibate for thirty years. And because sex has been off the table all along, we are able to be friends without having to guard against it.

After breakfast, we decide to drive into town. There is a tree Mot wants me to see. We drive around looking for it, circling a middle-class neighborhood near the University. While he drives, Mot tells me more about what's going on in his dreams, warning me.

"The Big Guys are trying to find a way to use this all to their advantage," he says, and I know that by "this all" he means me. "Watch out, because I don't always know what the program is. The Harpies warn me sometimes, but not all the time."

"The Big Guys Upstairs are the ones who really pull the strings," Mot says. If the Harpies are Mot's Greek chorus, these are the gods on Olympus who arbitrarily dictate the path of his days. "Jack" he says—pronouncing it "yok"—"is a likable guy. Sometimes I think he's the one you like, really. I don't know if you've ever really seen me." I don't either, so I keep my mouth shut. "Jack is the one who learned to tell time, played basketball in high school, had friends, and made people laugh. Anything likable, that's not me. That's Jack," Mot says. "Don't get tricked into thinking that's me, because that just means you'll end up being Jack's friend instead of mine. That's what always happens. Anything good I get, anything nice, they just take it."

Mot means this literally. I'm hungry and suggest stopping at Mazzola's Pizza, which we have passed three times in fifteen minutes, but we can't stop because Moloch, who lives in Mot's throat, is acting up and will steal the food from him as he swallows it and use it to feed The Others. There are days, maybe more than days, where Mot won't eat to try and starve Moloch out, but it never works. It only leaves Mot weak and feeling like yet another battle has been lost.

Finally, after passing the same landmarks a number of times, we go left where we had been going right and in a block or two come across a yard with an outrageous garden amid the green, watered lawns. Climbing aster grows extravagantly over a pergola on one side, morning glories over an arbor on the other. Between hollyhocks, dinner plate dahlias, tiger lilies, and dwarf sunflowers compete for attention in the explosion of color. There are no garden gnomes, no little wheelbarrows filled with begonias, but they are implied. "There is tacky yard art in the subtext of that garden," Mot jokes. "It is way over the top. Someone retired and went nuts!" He laughs and gestures out the driver's side window. Across the street, a catalpa tree blooms with more modest pastel flowers.

"It's lovely," I say, and it is. Next to the garish, ridiculous garden it looks perfect, every bloom exactly as it should be, the subtle shades outshining the garish colors of the dahlias and lilies. "Worth the drive." As if the drive itself weren't the point.

ON FRIDAY MORNING, MOT WAKES BELIEVING his only remaining sibling, a sister named Antoinette, has died. He knows this, he explains, because she's crying so loudly inside his head he can't hear me when I speak. Until today, she had not been one of the ones weeping in the background. Mot's angry with her sons for not notifying him. "How would they have found you?" I ask, and he doesn't know but isn't appeased. The impossible is a matter of course for him.

We decide to go out for some lunch and to see a movie. Mot is uncharacteristically adamant we see *Mr. Brooks*. I haven't heard anything about it, but he's seen the preview and insists. All I can tell from the ad is that William Hurt and Kevin Costner are in the cast and it is some sort of cop film. Not my sort of movie, really, but I'm not the one who needs to quiet the voices in my head, so I agree.

The theater is in a part of Amarillo we didn't know existed, a newer, wealthier part, where we discover all the chain restaurants and coffee houses we had thought were missing. On the drive, Mot talks about his family. He has talked about his family often enough, but its makeup is a muddle to me. I know he had four siblings. There was a brother who lived in the Pacific Northwest and seems to have done well until, in middle age, he killed himself. And, of course, the sister he believes has just died. Antoinette is the only one he ever names, so although he says, "my brother did this," or "my sister did that," there's no way to know which of them he means. I believe he had two brothers and two sisters, but it may have been three and one. Collectively, Mot refers to the five of them as *The Five Easy Pieces* and says they have been picked off one by one; he is the last left standing. Usually, I don't ask questions, I wait for him to tell me what he wants me to know. Today it feels possible to talk him out of believing his sister has died, so I press when I otherwise would not.

"So, why don't you and your sister speak anymore?" I ask him.

"I've told you," he says, and then for five minutes a disjointed explanation spills out of him—a mass of words with no meaning. The trick of tracking the names doesn't work at all. He forgets to use verbs; affirmative statements become negative ones mid-sentence; only half a word gets said before he's on to the next. Oddly, he doesn't seem to notice. Finally, he looks me in the eye and says, "See, it's like I told you before. Done deal. Never gonna listen, so I can't talk to them."

Unable to follow any of what he's just told me, I pose the question in a different way, hoping for an answer I can understand. "So, if I asked your sister why you don't speak, would she tell me the same thing?"

"No," he answers. "She'd probably tell you it was because I molested her when we were kids. That I was the one who ruined her life. That's what she tells everyone."

That's it; that's all he says. No denial. No explanation.

I look at the man who gentled me through my own fears after I was attacked, an incident that seems insignificant compared to what he's just confessed. It isn't that I don't know lives are complicated, or understand the cycle of abuse. This grown man is not responsible for anything that poor, broken child might have done. It's just that I can't put these two halves of him together and come up with a whole. I look for the boy in the old man, but can't see him at this distance, or maybe from this angle. He's told me his mother used to try to pinch off his penis when he was little, to make him the girl he was supposed to be, and he acknowledges but won't discuss other sexual abuses. This confession changes the meaning of these stories for me; my understanding of him is more complicated now. I try to turn him back into the Mot I knew this morning. But it's impossible not to reflect and look for hints of predation in his stories, to not be afraid of what I might have let into my life. Everything I have believed about him teeters on the fulcrum of a single answer.

I work up the nerve to ask the necessary question. "Have you ever touched another child?" I can't imagine what I will do if the answer is yes.

He looks at me, his gaze clear, not even surprised. "No. I mean I've always been attracted to younger people. I'm really a kid, never was allowed to develop into a real person like the rest of you, so it makes sense that I'm attracted to kids because that's as far as I ever got in life. But I know there's a line, and I've never crossed it. Just because They hit the old erection button and try to use sex to make me be like Them, doesn't mean I have to do it." I believe him, but I'm shaken, in part by how much delusion there is in his explanation. Can I trust as truth something so entwined with madness? It's a fragile faith; I have to work to hold on to it. But I am not ready to let my own cowardice be the thing that separates us.

At the theater, I excuse myself and go to the bathroom to splash water on my face and take a few moments alone to collect myself. *Mr. Brooks*, it turns out, is a movie about a serial killer with an imaginary friend who eggs him on. Costner plays the murderer; William Hurt plays Marshall, a character only Brooks can see, who goads an unwilling Brooks into the killings. After the first gruesome scene I tell Mot I want to leave. I say I don't think I'm up for this kind of movie just now. I don't tell him how brittle my faith in him is, or that I'm afraid the movie might shatter it. He points back to the screen and barks, "Watch it!" in a demanding tone I haven't heard before. "This is just like me; this is EXACTLY what it's like." He pauses for a minute, and adds, "Did you notice I said that in Hurt's voice? Sometimes he's one of the ones over here; he wants me to go to Hollywood to make movies and be one of *them*." I have no idea what this might mean, and I'm not asking.

On the drive back to the campground, I try to pull it together, but I can't. Mot chatters excitedly about the ways in which the movie mirrors his own experience, although he makes sure to say "except for all the killing" every few minutes after I tell him he's scaring me. Once again, I feel like the reasonable thing would be to just leave, pretend I'm worn out and want to start the drive back to Morgantown a little early.

Since this drive, I've been acutely aware of how little I really know about Mot. I may never have even met Tom, the person in whose body all of these gods, daemons, and regular Joes reside. I believe Mot knows there are boundaries and doesn't cross them, but I don't know if he speaks for the rest of Them, or if he even knows what the Others have or haven't done. I remember that he told me once, "They don't like Jews. I mean, I can think of at least one Jew who has died because of the bad guys over here." At the time I'd thought it was more delusion, or some reference to Kaiser Wilhelm when he was a living, real person. Now I don't know.

Mot is genuinely my friend, and I know the ways in which my world is better, less lonely, because of him. I am grateful to him for getting me through a very difficult period in my life, a time made harder than it should have been because it echoed events of sexual violence in my past. I don't want to run away from him in fear and I worry about what it would mean for him if I did. But what if Mot is just this sweet, naïve guy the Others throw up to get what they need from the world, taking him back down again when they feel like it? What if someday Moloch looks me straight in the eye and says, "We warned you." For a few hours, the world feels made of spun glass, everything on the verge of shattering.

WE GET TO THE CABIN SURPRISED AT HOW EARLY it still is; we don't have the strength for a day so long. I swim, Mot naps. The place is filled with weekend campers. The pool roils with children wound up by long car rides and haggard parents who toss themselves onto the deck chairs and shut their eyes. I wonder if my own fragile trust is enough to make it all right that I have brought Mot among them; I'm glad he is napping rather than swimming with me. I do not want to have to watch him watching the children play, or to wonder if the longing in his eyes is for his own lost childhood or something more sinister. My fear is an ugly, alien thing. I don't know how a friendship could survive it.

It's easy to identify the events that break us, harder to name the myriad tiny things that knit us back together. Saturday morning hurries by in a series of necessary tasks. We pack and load the cars so our last hours can be spent on better things. Mot sorts the camping gear and cleans the cabin while I do the laundry; together, we divide up what we've acquired over the week. He takes the coffee pot, the hotplate, and the leftover rice and lentils. I keep the straw basket and the wild alfalfa he harvested for a tea we never made. We make our last pilgrimage to Wal-Mart. Mot buys engine additives for my car that I think may do more harm than good but allow anyway. He accepts a cell phone from me, although he can't go so far as to promise he'll use it.

We spend our last evening quietly, reading to one another, making a meal of the last of the fruit, bread, and cheese bought during the week. He gets out the road atlas and marks good stopping places on my route home. I sew missing buttons onto his shirts.

I am awake by five, anxious to get the goodbye over with. I shower and get the last of my things together, then wake Mot. "I'm going now," I whisper, leaning over his head on the pillow. It's the first time I've crossed the invisible barrier between his side of the cabin and mine in all the time we've been here.

He walks groggily to the porch with me, rubbing his eyes and obviously surprised to see that it's still dark, but he doesn't suggest I put off leaving.

"I left the key in the drop box by the office, but you don't have to leave until eleven. Feel free to go back to bed. I just need to get on the road."

I step off the porch and turn back to face him, car keys in my hand. He looks down at me, takes my face in his good hand, and kisses me lightly on the forehead. "Drive safely," he says, and then, looking over the top of my head at the darkened horizon, "I think I would love you if They let me feel love. This is probably the closest I'll get."

I smile and get into my car. It's a long drive home. As I pull away, Mot's still standing on the porch, staring out at the big sky.

Going to Ground

Like a good citizen, I call my senators at least once a week these days, but their aides are brusque. They tell me that Alexander and Corker support the President's education agenda/healthcare reform/immigration order or whatever I'm outraged about on that day. In the first few weeks, they'd thank me for my call. Now they simply say, "Your objection is noted," and hang up as quickly as they can. Once, as if caught off guard, one said, "Are you sure you live in Tennessee?"

I carry my passport with me everywhere these days.

I've begun to sort that which is precious from that which is not. I make a small pile of the things I'd pack in the night, a larger one of the stuff I would leave. Everyone is insisting we're just one Reichstag Fire away from fascism. On the news, I watch a steady stream of black people murdered by the state for their blackness, and I think it's more likely that we've already had the Anschluss.

When I travel, I wear an inherited diamond I feel silly wearing at home. I remember being told when I was younger that a Jewish woman should always have enough jewelry on her body to bribe her way over a border. At the time it seemed quaint. Now it seems key. For the moment, the diamond ring's still on my finger. I wonder if there will come a day I'll need to sew it into the hem of my coat.

Over coffee, my friend Meredith talks about joining the resistance in a way that suggests we're headed for a war she thinks we can win. I talk about going to ground, about building false walls for hiding people waiting for fake passports and safe transport. We scare ourselves and then laugh at ourselves, but even after the laughing we are still scared.

Meredith wasn't always Meredith, and there is a passel of bills in our state legislature designed to make it impossible for her to be Meredith now. I tell her I will hide her in my hidden rooms, if it comes to that. She says she won't be hidden, but she might move to Atlanta.

My coffee these days is chamomile tea. I'm jittery enough as it is.

If we flee, we will go to my husband's family in Austria. The irony of this is not lost on me; there are Nazis in the family albums. They assure us that we'll be safe there, should it come to that, and I believe them. They've clearly learned lessons that we have not.

My husband has stopped talking about becoming an American citizen and started talking about being an anchor relative.

My friend Jessica is spending all her vacation time in Israel this year, establishing the Right of Return. I've stopped questioning the politics of this; refugees go where they can.

This Hanukkah, I will give my niece and nephews passports if they don't already have them. If they do, I will give them whatever they ask for. I've lifted my moratorium on war toys. Maybe they should know how to handle a gun.

My closest disabled friends and I swap lists of medications and start to horde the things one or some of us need against the day we lose access to them. We read up on actual expiration versus labeled expiration dates. We refill prescriptions before we need to, just in case.

I have six boxes of Plan B in my closet, even though I'm long past childbearing years. On campus, I spread rumors about a shadowy network of old women who will help younger women with travel and money for abortions if they can't get the healthcare they need in their hometowns. I call all my old woman friends and build the network. I keep their names and numbers in handwritten lists and hide them away.

I refuse to let my husband put a "Stop Trump" bumper sticker on our car. "That's just foolish," I say. I let him keep the Cthulhu fish. For now.

A young woman cries in my office, afraid that if she comes out to her parents they will disown her; she's still dependent on them. I tell her that she doesn't have to come out to them now, or ever, if she doesn't feel safe doing so. She looks shocked. It breaks my heart to have been the first to suggest the safety of the closet to her; I wonder what she is coming out of, if it had never occurred to her to remain in.

I've stopped going to protests and started going to meetings for which there are no flyers or Facebook event notices. To find them, you have to know someone who already has. We talk there of things I won't write here. At first, we turned off our phones. Now, we leave them at home.

And yet still, like a good citizen, I call my senators at least once a week. Their aides are brusque. In the first few weeks, they'd thank me for my call. Now they hang up as quickly as they can. I haven't yet given up on the dream of America, but I'm making contingency plans.

On Marriage

My love is sick today, and so it's all soup made with bone broth and time on the couch, piles of tissues and nests of blankets. Both open windows and a fire in the fireplace. Only the sounds of tea kettles and turning pages.

The sun is bright on this rare clear day in what has been a grey December. The crows on the lawn abide by the silence we are keeping, they peck but do not caw. A cat prowls along the garden fence, silent also because that's the way with cats. It keeps a respectful distance from the crows.

Yesterday there was separate visiting with separate friends; mine a town away, his down at the game store. Later, there was wine at home with a little television. *It's good*, I said, *that we are so comfortable doing things without the other*. I'd once been in a marriage where that wasn't allowed. *Yes*, he said, *but the best part of the day is when we are home again together*. And I trust this, although I was also once in a marriage where that wasn't true.

The kettle is on again. I'll brew feverfew and ephedra, stinging nettle and lemon balm from the wild tangle of weeds we call our garden. He'll wrinkle his nose when I bring the cup, but drink it, then ask for a cup of proper tea as if it's a reward he's earned.

Tomorrow, he'll tell me *I feel mostly better now* whether he feels better at all or not, and I'll press my lips against his forehead to test for fever, hold his hand to see if it's clammy, check his eyes to see if they are bright. And if he is fevered or clammy or dull, I will say *Stay on the couch another day, just to be sure*. I will make his rest a favor to me, so that he can have it. So that he will not get up to do the vacuuming or take out the trash or do some other thing that either I can do or we can leave undone. *Alright*, he'll say, with a sigh. *Though I really do feel better*. Whether he does or not. *But if you think it's best*.

And on the day after tomorrow, he'll tell me *I really am all better now* whether he is or not, and I'll press my lips against his forehead, hold his hand, check his eyes. And even if there is a fever, or his eyes are dull, I will say *Well, if you really think you are, maybe we could do a few things today, but nothing too strenuous, okay?* And if there is a fever I will bring out the bills and write the checks while he rests on the couch, so that we can say we've gotten something done. I will take the trash out to the curb, which really I could do all the time, though it's nice that he does it for us. I will vacuum the house even though it disturbs his napping, because so does the dust in the corners. There is only so much quiet, so much rest, that we can bear. On the day after tomorrow, we will have our fill.

But today my love is sick, and so it's all soup made with bone broth and time on the couch, piles of tissues and nests of blankets. Both open windows and a fire in the fireplace. Only the sounds of tea kettles and turning pages.

Striking the Match

My husband gets up in the middle of the night to go to the bathroom. In the moonlight, his long blond hair looks almost white, his skin glows. I lie quietly and stare at the small of his back, the curve of his ass, the delicate taper of his thighs. This is a kind of looking that, until I married him, I knew only how to receive, not to give; a looking that is full of desire for the other, not as a whole being, but as an object of beauty.

This is not how he looks at me. I'm on the cusp of fifty and look it. He's on the cusp of forty and doesn't. My body has aged hard and I've not treated it well. Even in my youth, I was plain, perhaps pretty for a year or two in my early twenties and maybe again a little elegant during a stretch of good months in my thirties but being beautiful has always been beyond me. If people find me so, it's only after they've come to know me. I have never turned heads. I minded this quite a lot in my teens, when it seemed that only beautiful people mattered, that it was a prerequisite for a good life. But it isn't, and it didn't take too many years out in the world to realize that it's more important to be interesting than beautiful, and interesting is something I can manage.

I once dated a woman so beautiful that she glided through life on the desire of others. A man she didn't sleep with paid her rent and, although she wasn't an artist, called himself her *patron*. Another man she didn't sleep with had given her a car. "Someone needs to take care of you," he'd said to her, though the car itself proved she was savvier about the way of the world than he was. "Someone like you needs looking after." Bartenders covered her tab, drug dealers never asked for their money, policemen always let her go with a warning.

I tried to look at her then the way I look at my husband now, but her beauty nettled me. The way she wielded it discomfited me. I'd seen how she treated the people who desired her, and I didn't want to make myself that sort of fool. It's a dangerous way to look at someone who does not love you.

My husband is honest enough to say that he has never found my body particularly desirable, but still he asked me out on our first date three years ago because he found my way of being in the world, my sense of humor, and my intelligence sexy. *That matters more*, he says, *and makes you beautiful to me*. Sometimes that *to me* breaks my heart a little bit; sometimes it makes me feel loved.

It took us a while to arrive at this understanding. It was only once I thought to ask, *do you not find my body sexy?* instead of simply, *don't you find me sexy?* that he could articulate the difference. These weren't conversations we wanted to have, but they were necessary. And I know that it's our ability to talk about the hard things that is really the strength of our marriage, that this matters far more than who reaches for whom in the night.

Still, it's taken some getting used to, this being the one who desires rather than the one who is desired. Being the one to say, *I want you*. The one to extend the goodnight kiss beyond *sleep well* and into *let me touch you*. The one who mutters in the middle of it, *my god, you are beautiful*. The one who sometimes whispers, *thank you.* The one who afterwards makes up the outside part of the spoon.

It would be a lie to say that I never miss the flash of longing in a lover's eye, the low growl of desire near my ear during lovemaking, the thrill of being wanted, urgently, by someone. The opportunity to say *yes* instead of to ask, *would you?* The quiet pleasure of acquiescence to someone else's need.

A man I know only a little sits next to me in our local coffeehouse. He looks at the title of the book I'm reading, which just happens to be Jack Halberstam's *Female Masculinity,* and says in a low voice, *I never can figure out if you academics make everything sexy, or if you take all the sexiness out of everything.* By the way he leans in further than he needs to when he speaks and holds my eyes after he's done, I recognize that he's making a pass. It occurs to me that he may not know that I'm married; he's only the friend of a friend, and I've stopped wearing my ring because I tend to fidget with it in a way that gets on even my nerves. So I smile and say, *It's probably a little bit of both* in my flirty voice and lean in for just a moment to enjoy the sparkle in his eye, the way he's looking at me. But then I lean away again and say, *But, really, it's probably more of the latter* because I am married, happily so, and have gotten everything I want from this encounter.

In our early days, before my husband could articulate the ways in which he both did, and did not, feel desire for me, we sometimes fought about our sex life. *I'm tired of always having to be the one who makes the first move,* I'd say, and *do you think I'm ugly,* and of course *are you sure you love me?* And he would say *I'll try to be better about that* and *of course not* and *more than anything, because you're my person.* And we'd make love that night because he'd reach for me, and then not again—sometimes for weeks—until I reached for him.

In my mid-twenties, I had an affair with a man who had just turned sixty. He was not a handsome man, but he was kind and funny. When we were in bed together, he would marvel at the smoothness of my skin, the tautness of my muscles, the rise of my breasts, and the tiny swell of my belly. He could lie beside me for hours at a time, just tracing the length of my spine with his fingers and whispering, *you are spring come to sweeten my old age.* And although I didn't find his body sexy, I craved his touch and the way he looked at me, amazed, as if my body were a gift I brought to him each time we lay together. It was a good love, and for many years we were happy until life took me to places where he couldn't follow.

I tell my husband, *I'm writing an essay about what it's like to be a person who is older and plain married to a person who is younger and beautiful. About what it's like to be married to someone who doesn't find my body sexy.* Part of me wants him to say, *Don't be ridiculous, you are beautiful and of course I think you're sexy* but instead he says, *I love you.* I read him the paragraphs that were hardest to write and say, *does this sound fair to you?* He says *yes* when some part of me had been wishing he would say *no.* On another day, it might scare me that we are so free to say these things, that they feel so immutably part of how we are together. Today, though, it's a relief. I have seen other women turn over their lives to hiding the truth of their aging, chasing the desire of a man, and I have neither the time nor the inclination for that. This is my body, and I live in it more happily than I would endure the awful things I'd need to do to make it appear young again; the plastic surgeries and starvation diets, the trips to the salon and the cosmetic dentistry. Where the years weigh heavily on me, it is because they were good years lived well, and I have no desire to make my history invisible.

The afternoon sun filters through the blinds and illuminates my husband where he lies in our bed after our lovemaking. His fine long legs and his delicate hands stick out from the tangle of our blankets, and he rests his head on my shoulder. *I love you,* he says, and I trust this. *I love you, too,* I say, and wrap my arms around his shoulders. And, although this is not the passion I am used to, it's still passion, and the heat of it is not diminished simply because I was the one who struck the match.

A Young Man Tells Me

. . . that he's fallen in love with the honey-haired girl in our class, and that if it's okay with me, he'd like not to have to talk today because now he's afraid he might say something dumb.

. . . that he feels helpless in the face of so much injustice in the world, and that he wonders what he can do to try to make things better. I invite him into my office and make him a cup of tea.

. . . that when he was a child, his father used to punch him in the arm when he cried, saying "Don't be such a pussy," and that he thinks the problem is that the rest of us are snowflakes who could use a good punch now and then to toughen us up.

. . . that he cries every time that damn animal rescue commercial comes on TV.

. . . that his Confederate flag t-shirt is about cultural pride, not racism.

. . . that when he told his father he is gay, his father threw up.

. . . that when he told his father he is gay, his father wrapped him in a bear hug and said, "I love you."

. . . that he will never tell his father he is gay.

. . . that he's thinking about dropping out of school because he's just so damn depressed.

. . . that he sleeps in his car most nights now because his roommate has bought a pistol and likes to hold it while he sits on the couch and drinks Jim Beam. "It's legal," says the young man, "so what can I do? But the lease runs out in a few months, and then I'm out of there."

. . . that he thinks I'm a Jewish radical who uses the university to brainwash good Christians and turn them into Marxists. He's read all about people like me on the Internet, he says.

. . . that his parents called to tell him they'd had to put down his dog, and he knows she was old, but he wishes they'd waited until Saturday when he could have driven home to say goodbye.

. . . that only his grandmother still calls him Scooter.

. . . that once, when he was about twelve, he hit the homerun that won a championship, and he worries that maybe he peaked at that moment.

. . . that dominance is hard-wired into us—some junk science about lobsters and serotonin—and this is why he's so aggressive. "It's like you want us all to be cucks," he says about my policy of politeness in the classroom. "Alphas gotta alpha."

. . . that he cries at night with a pillow over his head so his roommate can't hear him.

. . . that he wants to share the Good News of the Lord with me. I invite him into my office and make him a cup of tea.

. . . that I don't want to know what he saw in Afghanistan, but that if I did know it would break my heart. I tell him that my heart is indeed broken for him, and that I wish he'd never seen those things. "I say *saw*," he says, "but I mean *did*." I tell him that I know and reach out to put a hand on his arm, but he flinches away.

. . . that he missed class last week because he'd checked himself into rehab, but then his parents told him that if he didn't finish the semester, they were done with him, so he checked himself back out and he wonders whether he can do some extra credit to make up for the points he missed while he was gone. I tell him that there's no need, but he says, "No, no. I was raised to be responsible. Missing class is on me. What do I need to do to make it right?"

. . . that I remind him of his grandmother, of whom he is fond

. . . that I'm a fat bitch.

. . . that when he was small he saw the ghost of his grandfather hovering over his bed, and that all these years later he still looks for that ghost every night before he falls asleep even though he's never seen it again.

. . . that he found Jesus the night he totaled his truck, drunk on grain alcohol and grape juice from a high school party, and that although it was worth it because salvation is more important than material things, he really misses that truck.

. . . that once he found a wallet with two hundred bucks in it, and although he was sorely tempted, he returned it to the address on the driver's license inside. When he knocked on the door, the elderly white man who answered kept the chain on even as he reached out for the wallet. He says, "And I bet that old man would insist he isn't a racist." I can only nod.

. . . that I've left my keys in my office door again.

. . . that his girlfriend is pregnant and they don't know what to do. I invite him into my office and make him a cup of tea.

. . . that his mother says I'm full of shit, that his short stories are brilliant and don't need any revision.

. . . that when he was very small, the Voice of God told him to be a preacher when he grew up, but he's terrified of speaking in front of people, which he thought he'd grow out of but hasn't, and so he's now also terrified of disappointing God.

. . . that he's writing a book about a boy who finds out he's the chosen one, goes on a quest, and eventually becomes the king of all the land.

. . . that someone touched him in a way that was wrong when he was small, and that he's been through therapy and is mostly OK, but that he just couldn't read the book I'd assigned and he hopes I understand. I do.

. . . that everyone thinks only girls have it hard.

. . . that sometimes he wishes he were a girl.

. . . that he can't wait to be a man.

PUBLICATION ACKNOWLEDGMENTS

Self-Portrait in Apologies was originally published in *Fringe Magazine*

The Origins of My Problems with Fidelity (unpublished)

A Meditation on Love was originally published in *The Fiddleback*

Fearsome Beauty was originally published in *Fringe Magazine*

The Way Things Go was originally published in *Whitefish Review*

Almost Home was originally published in *Creative Nonfiction*

Shelter was originally published in *The Sun*

What I Know of Madness was originally published *r.kv.r.y quarterly literary journal*

When I Lived in Manhattan was originally published in *Fringe Magazine*

Mot was originally published in *Ninth Letter*

Going to Ground was originally published in *Full Grown People*

On Marriage was originally published in *Still: The Journal*

Striking the Match was originally published in the anthology *Soul Mate 101 and Other Essays on Love and Sex*

A Young Man Tells Me was originally published in *Booth*

AUTHOR BIO

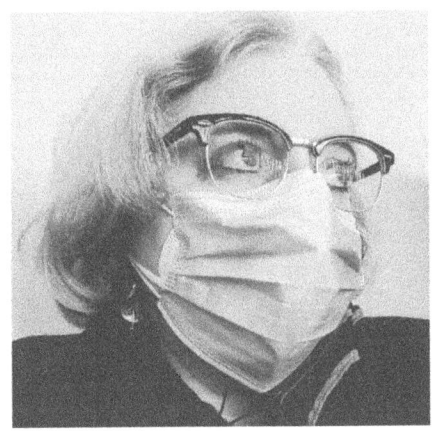

Sarah Einstein is a native of Huntington, West Virginia and comes home as often as she can. She teaches creative writing at the University of Tennessee at Chattanooga. She is the author of *Mot: A Memoir* (University of Georgia Press, 2015) and *Remnants of Passion* (SheBooks, 2014). Her essays and short stories have appeared in *The Sun Magazine, Ninth Letter, PANK,* and other journals. Her work has been reprinted in the *Best of the Net* and awarded a Pushcart Prize and the AWP Prize for Creative Nonfiction.

www.ingramcontent.com/pod-product-compliance
Ingram Content Group UK Ltd.
Pitfield, Milton Keynes, MK11 3LW, UK
UKHW021326180426
11947UKWH00017B/1463